· PHILIP PULLMAN'S

His Dark Materials Trilogy

A READER'S GUIDE

CLAIRE SQUIRES

CONTINUUM | NEW YORK | LONDON

2003

The Continuum International Publishing Group Inc
15 E 26 Street, New York, NY 10010

The Continuum International Publishing Group Ltd
The Tower Building, 11 York Road, London SE1 7NX

www.continuumbooks.com

Printed in the United States of America

Library of Congress Cataloging-in-Publication Data

Squires, Claire.
  Philip Pullman's His dark materials trilogy : a reader's guide /
Claire Squires.
    p.   cm.
  Includes bibliographical references and index.
  ISBN 0-8264-1479-6 (alk. paper)
  1. Pullman, Philip, 1946– His dark materials.   2. Young adult fiction,
English — History and criticism.   3. Fantasy fiction, English — History
and criticism.   I. Title: His dark materials trilogy.   II. Title.
PR6066.U44H57   2003
823'.914 — dc21   2003008918

ISBN 0-8264-1479-6

Philip Pullman's
His Dark Materials Trilogy

CONTINUUM CONTEMPORARIES

Also available in this series:

Contents

Acknowledgements

With many thanks to everyone who has helped in the writing of this guide. I would particularly like to thank Philip Pullman, David Barker at Continuum, Rosie Holland, Kirstie Blair, Matthew Creasy, Beccy Loncraine, Michael and Christine Squires, and the Oxford Contemporary Writing Reading Group.

Note on the Texts

The page references to *Northern Lights* (NL), *The Subtle Knife* (SK) and *The Amber Spyglass* (AS) are to the UK paperback editions.

1

The Novelist

If Philip Pullman's dazzling, lengthy and complex *His Dark Materials* has one message above all others, it is this: *"tell them stories"* (AS, p. 456). For Lyra, the protagonist of the entire trilogy, storytelling is her great power, leading her in and out of hair-raising adventures, and eventually toward the responsibility of adulthood. For Mary Malone, the nun-turned-physicist, her narrative of sexual experience and loss of faith is the spur to Lyra's great destiny. For those trapped in the underworld, storytelling is the ultimate redemption, the means by which they will escape the land of the dead into a joyful reunion with the living world.

His Dark Materials is told by a master storyteller, Philip Pullman. At 1,300 pages of closely-plotted story, *Northern Lights* (1995; published in the US as *The Golden Compass*), *The Subtle Knife* (1997) and *The Amber Spyglass* (2000), the three novels that make up the trilogy, have had an extraordinary critical and commercial success, as well as achieving with the final volume what no children's book had ever previously done: winning a major literary prize—the Whitbread Book of the Year Award—in competition with books for adults.

The importance of storytelling within the trilogy is paralleled, then, by the dexterity of Pullman's own narrative.

Born in Norwich on 19 October 1946, Pullman's early childhood followed the itinerant route of his RAF father's career. Journeying between postings was by sea—giving Pullman the chance, at a very young age, to begin his storytelling vocation by entertaining his younger brother on the long voyages. The family lived in Southern Rhodesia (now Zimbabwe) for several years, before the death of his fighter-pilot father in an air crash in Kenya, while in combat against Mau Mau terrorists. Pullman, then, was made a "half-orphan," as he has put it, in the tradition of children's literature, and of his own heroes and heroines. Yet Pullman does not talk of this early tragedy as a devastating occurrence for him, but as a distanced one—his father was a glamorous but removed figure from his children's lives. After their father's death, the two boys went to live for a while with their maternal grandparents in Norfolk. This period was influential to Pullman: his grandfather was a Church of England clergyman, and also a great storyteller. As a child Pullman was surrounded by the narratives of the Bible, and by the linguistic heritage of the Church—the King James Bible and the Book of Common Prayer.

His mother remarried another RAF officer, and the family moved to Australia. This was another place that richly fed his imagination through the imports of American comics such as *Batman* and *Superman*, and the Australian radio dramas whose stories Pullman would extemporize on for himself and his brother. The interest in illustration and graphic novels that started with reading comics never left Pullman—he has written about illustration, incorporated his own illustrations into novels (including in *His Dark Materials*), worked closely with illustrators in other books, and in fact has expressed regret that he went to university rather than art school.

Eventually the family returned to the UK, and Pullman attended secondary school in Harlech, North Wales. During his adolescence, he started to write poetry, influenced by Dylan Thomas and the Metaphysical poets. Although he now concentrates on prose, Pullman sees this poetry-writing period as formative. "Rhythm is profoundly important," he says (in "An Introduction to . . . Philip Pullman"), and it is through the formal discipline of poetic structure that his "command of prose" developed. It was also at school, while studying for his A Levels, that he first read John Milton's epic poem *Paradise Lost* (1667), a text that would, years later, play a crucial role in the development of the plot of *His Dark Materials*. At the time, *Paradise Lost* struck Pullman for its deeply resonant poetic language, a language that still profoundly impresses him. The teacher at his school who introduced him to these early literary influences is paid due respect by Pullman. She is acknowledged at the end of *The Amber Spyglass*, for "the best that education can give, the notion that responsibility and delight can co-exist" (AS, p. 550), themes that also imbue *His Dark Materials*.

In 1965, Pullman went to the University of Oxford to read English. Exeter, his college, would later be transmuted into the Jordan College of Lyra's Oxford in *His Dark Materials*. The two colleges are located in the same geographical space, but Pullman turns his college into the biggest, and richest, Oxford college in *Northern Lights*. When Pullman talks about the legacy of Oxford in his work, and being a student at that famous university, what he tends to describe are not the tutorials he attended, or the books he read, but the strange rituals of college life, and of evenings spent precariously climbing over the rooftops: scenes that would be incorporated into the opening chapters of *Northern Lights* (see Pullman's article "Dreaming of Spires" for more on this).

After graduating from Oxford, Pullman had various jobs including a spell working at the gentleman's outfitters, Moss Bros., in London. Although he already planned to write books, and indeed had an adult novel, *The Haunted Storm*, published by 1972 (which he claims to be "terrible"), he decided to train to be a teacher, and took a teaching diploma in Weymouth. He then returned to Oxford, where he has lived ever since, to teach in middle schools (for children aged 9 to 13).

This was another highly formative period for Pullman. At the time, the school curriculum was very open, allowing Pullman to concentrate on what he liked best, and discovered he was best at: storytelling. He recounted Greek myths to his classes, with Homer's *The Iliad* and *The Odyssey* being particular favorites for his retellings. He also wrote plays for his pupils to perform, which would later become novels in their own right: *Count Karlstein* (1982), *The Ruby in the Smoke* (1985) and *The Firework Maker's Daughter* (1995) were all conceived in this way. It is perhaps in writing for a dual audience for these plays—for the child performers and watchers, and for their parents—that he began to experiment with the incorporation of various levels of narration and meaning in his texts, a facet which would become very important with *His Dark Materials*. More than anything, though, Pullman sees his time as a schoolteacher as one in which he refined his *oral* storytelling skills, in a tradition stretching all the way back to "Homer and the bards" ("An Introduction to . . . Philip Pullman").

While a schoolteacher, Pullman was seconded to Westminster College to set up a center to co-ordinate language teaching in the region. Later, he was made a lecturer at the college, teaching child and adult literature. During this period, after publishing a second novel for adults, *Galatea* (1978), Pullman began to write for children, and his growing success, which would culminate with the publication of the *His Dark Materials* trilogy, allowed him to become a full-time writer.

The two early, adult, novels published by Pullman are neither widely available now, nor generally discussed by critics in relation to his later successes. Pullman himself, while professing an affection for *Galatea*, dismisses them both as youthful, and flawed, works. Yet their concerns are ones which would later come to be taken up in *His Dark Materials*. *The Haunted Storm* is a weird narrative concerning murder and incest, and features a Gnostic cleric and a 23-year-old ridden by existential angst. While its portrayal of perverted sexuality would hardly recommend it to a child who had enjoyed *Northern Lights*, *The Subtle Knife* and *The Amber Spyglass*, its quest for religious knowledge is also central to *His Dark Materials*. *Galatea*, a picaresque, magic realist tale, similar in structure and style to fantastical work such as Angela Carter's *The Infernal Desire Machines of Doctor Hoffman* (1972), is populated by a profusion of characters including zombies, automata and "Electric Whores." The array of beings is reminiscent of the teeming populations of different worlds in *The Amber Spyglass*.

The children's books that followed these two early adult works can be broadly split into three categories. The first are stories of adventure, including the series of novels set in Victorian England and starring Sally Lockhart and her friends. The atmosphere evoked by the novels' location is similar to the London of Charles Dickens, Wilkie Collins and Leon Garfield. *The Ruby in the Smoke*, *The Shadow in the North* (1988; originally published as *The Shadow in the Plate*), *The Tiger in the Well* (1991) and *The Tin Princess* (1994), are in many ways forerunners of the *His Dark Materials* trilogy. They are tales of high adventure, with independent young people as the protagonists who must use their virtues of bravery, loyalty and resourcefulness to overcome evil. The characters, though not as young as Will and Lyra, have unsettled family backgrounds: when Sally is first introduced she is a 16-year-old orphan whose unconventional upbringing leads her to confront the mores of her society, initially by setting up her own business, and then by becoming an unmarried mother. Upon the young shoulders of these characters, who are coming to terms with questions of moral responsibility, their sexual feelings, and treachery in many forms, lies an urgent need to defeat wrongdoing, to protect the disadvantaged, and even to juggle with the destinies of states. In this series, Pullman, while spinning fast-paced yarns of high excitement, is uncompromising in his refusal to provide happy endings: in *The Shadow in the North* one of the heroes is killed, and *The Tin Princess* closes with a violent scene of twisted love, where innocence and experience collide in a dreadful fate.

The Tiger in the Well has a character with a prototype for the dæmons of *His Dark Materials*. Yet this proto-dæmon—a servant-monkey—is not the playful companion that Pantalaimon is to Lyra, but an emanation of the brooding, sick, malign presence of its owner. The monkey appears to many as a supernatural being, "a little imp from hell that waits on him" (p. 26). The Sally Lockhart series also privileges storytelling: it is the narratives of nationhood, for example, that Adelaide calls upon when she becomes ruler of Razkavia in *The Tin Princess*, and for the badly injured Daniel Goldberg, faced by a hostile, anti-Semitic crowd, it is both a lifesaver and a clarion call to racial tolerance in *The Tiger in the Well*:

And Goldberg felt a moment of pure, clear-headed elation. It was a kind of religious glee: holy mischief. He was weak with loss of blood, he was exhausted, his arm throbbed with an abominable pain, and there was an armed crowd in front of him that the slightest miscalculation would send mad. He thought: is there anywhere else I'd rather be? Anything else I'd rather be doing now than this?

What a lucky bugger I am, he said to himself. Talk for your life, Danny boy. Tell 'em a story. (p. 347)

Daniel's bravery in the face of danger and, moreover, his love of the challenge of talking for his life, align him with Pullman's parade of storytellers, which culminate in the figure of Lyra.

Storytelling is also central to *Clockwork or All Wound Up* (1996), one of the second category of works that Pullman describes as "(longish) fairy tales" (in "An Introduction to . . . Philip Pullman"). These include rewritings of existing tales—*I Was a Rat . . . or The Scarlet Slippers* (1999) has as its protagonist a pageboy-rat who fails to make it back to Cinderella's carriage on time—or original stories drawing on fairy and folk traditions. Set in a little German town during a hard winter, *Clockwork* is populated by folk tale-like characters and situations. It is a metanarrative, telling stories within stories that comment upon the responsibilities of the storyteller, and using the inexorable clockwork mechanism as a metaphor for the unstoppable powers of story.

In all of these "fairy tales," but particularly in *Clockwork*, *I Was a Rat* and *Spring-Heeled Jack: A Story of Bravery and Evil* (1989), illustration is an important storytelling device. In these books Pullman worked closely with the illustrators Peter Bailey and David Mostyn so that the pictures both tell the story, and comment upon it. The multilayered narration of these illustrated fairy tales demonstrates Pullman's awareness of the different audiences for his book, so that in *I Was a Rat!*, for example, there is a satirical commentary upon tabloid journalism's influence on popular opinion that would appeal to children and adults differently.

As with the Sally Lockhart series, these "fairy tales" are populated with resourceful children or young adults bereft of adult supervision. They encounter challenges that require them to think quickly but remain loyal, and above all to be brave. A moral universe develops in these books that has nothing to do with convention, laws, or society's mores. This is the morality made explicit in the didactic conclusion to *The Amber Spyglass*.

Realist teen novels make the third category of Pullman's books, although elements of the supernatural and adventure still intrude: *The Broken Bridge* (1990) features a teenage girl's search for her Haitian mother, and *The Butterfly Tattoo* (1992; originally published as *The White Mercedes*) is a thriller set in Oxford. Pullman has also published versions of *The Wonderful World of Aladdin and the Enchanted Lamp* (1995), *Mossycoat* (1998) and *Puss in Boots* (2000), as well as a variety of play adaptations, including *Frankenstein* (1990) from Mary Shelley's 1818 novel, and *Sherlock Holmes and the Limehouse Horror* (1990), which takes Arthur Conan Doyle's detective on a new adventure.

Pullman has continued to live in Oxford with his wife and two sons. The influence of the city as a setting in Pullman's writing is apparent from reading *His Dark Materials*, in which the real-life locations of Will's Oxford and the imaginatively rewrought ones of Lyra's provide much of the backdrop of the trilogy. One scene in *The Subtle Knife*, for example, has Lyra discovering trepanned skulls in the Pitt Rivers Museum in Will's Oxford, a location that is also integral to Penelope Lively's *The House in Norham Gardens* (1974). The final chapter of the trilogy is set in Oxford's Botanic Garden. Oxford's esoteric rituals, its august tradition as a seat of learning, its occasional insertion into British history as a place of political and religious treachery, and the unsurpassed beauty of its architecture, all contribute to making it a city attractive to the creative mind. Indeed, Oxford has been a home to some of Britain's most distinguished and vividly imaginative writers of children's books, including Lewis Carroll (author of *Alice's Adventures in Wonderland* (1865)), C. S. Lewis (author of the *Chronicles of Narnia* (1950–56) and J. R. R. Tolkein (author of *The Hobbit* (1937) and *The Lord of the Rings* (1954–5)).

Many have claimed that Pullman has joined this distinguished tradition with *His Dark Materials*, and comparisons have particularly been made with the *Chronicles of Narnia* and *The Lord of the Rings*. All three series undoubtedly share a comprehensive vision that creates a world, or parallel worlds, of great imaginative depth. Yet Pullman has been emphatic in denying similarities between his work and these earlier authors, on two specific grounds. The first is to do with genre description, and the second is concerned with attitudes toward religion and adolescence.

Tolkein is the acknowledged master of fantasy fiction. Pullman's trilogy is also arguably a work of fantasy, defined in *The Oxford Companion to English Literature* (2000) as a "liberation from the constraints of what is known, coupled with a plausible and persuasive inner coherence." *His Dark Materials* certainly displays such characteristics: a knife that can cut between worlds, a vehicle that works by thought-power alone, humans accompanied by daemons. In interview, however, Pullman has stated that "*Northern Lights* is not a fantasy. It's a work of stark realism" (in "Talking to Philip Pullman" by Wendy Parsons and Catriona Nicholson). Such a pronouncement is contentious—the reality of the worlds encountered in *His Dark Materials* is very different to that of our world—but perhaps what Pullman is suggesting is the conflict between fantasy and psychological realism. Elsewhere he has dismissed Tolkein's writing for being "'not interesting psychologically; there's nothing about people in it'" (in Helena de Bertodano, "I am of the Devil's Party," *Sunday Telegraph*). The claim of "stark realism" for his work is Pullman's way of promoting his own skill in developing character motivation: although the worlds of *His Dark Materials* may be unknown to us, the psychological manner in which characters traverse them is instantly recognizable. In fact, the series of children's books to which Pullman gives the most praise is the *Swallows and Amazons* series (1930–47) by Arthur Ransome: only fantastical today in the freedom that is given to the child protagonists to adventure in the realist landscapes of the Lake District, the Norfolk Broads, and the sea.

Although these debates over genre and character motivation are highly relevant, Pullman's argument with C. S. Lewis is a yet more urgent one. Pullman has repeatedly attacked Lewis's *Chronicles of Narnia* for their "pernicious" influence (see "Talking to Philip Pullman"). In "The Dark Side of Narnia," an article published in the

Guardian in 1998, Pullman criticized his predecessor in the strongest of terms. The series is "one of the most ugly and poisonous things I've ever read," to be vilified for "the misogyny, the racism, the sadomasochistic relish for violence that permeates [it]." More than any of these crimes, though, what Pullman contests is the Christian allegory of the *Chronicles*, and their very negative treatment of adolescence. The final volume, *The Last Battle* (1956), is heavily criticized by Pullman for its assertion that the ultimate reward is to be found in heaven rather than on earth, and for its exclusion of one of the characters from salvation because of her teenage—and female— interest in stockings and make-up. The *Chronicles'* distaste for adolescent sexuality provides a foil to Pullman's contrasting treatment of the same theme in *His Dark Materials*, and to compare the two series is ultimately to establish their very different moral stance. Pullman has also set *His Dark Materials* against Lewis's treatment of the myth of the Fall in his adult science fiction title *Perelandra* [*Voyage to Venus*] (1943).

For his pronouncements on the *Chronicles of Narnia*, and also for the attacks made both in the text of *His Dark Materials* itself as well as in interviews and speeches on the Christian Church and its legacy of violence and oppression, Pullman has made enemies. The *Catholic Herald* infamously described *The Amber Spyglass* as "worthy of the bonfire" and "the stuff of nightmares." Peter Hitchens, writing in the *Mail on Sunday*, labeled him "the most dangerous author in Britain" for his condemnation of Lewis and the Church. Pullman's criticism of organized religion is investigated in the next chapter, and the debate about Lewis and religion is further addressed in Chapter Three.

Paradise Lost is another source of religious narrative and imagery in *His Dark Materials*. Pullman describes his intent in writing the trilogy as "*Paradise Lost* for teenagers in three volumes"—a comment initially made half in jest, but then converted to reality (see

"Talking to Philip Pullman"). In the Acknowledgements to the trilogy (which appear at the end of *The Amber Spyglass*), Pullman mentions his allegiances, and his propensity to intertextuality: "I have stolen ideas from every book I have ever read." (*AS*, p. 549) Three acknowledgements are made above all others, one of which is to *Paradise Lost*: indeed the title of the trilogy comes from a line in *Paradise Lost*, which is used as the epigraph to *Northern Lights*.

In *Paradise Lost*, Milton recasts the Biblical story of the temptation of Eve and the fall of man in epic poetry. Yet Milton develops the narrative beyond the frame provided by Genesis, the first book of the Bible, and portrays a fully imagined cosmos in which the fallen angels, and Satan—Eve's tempter—are set against the autocratic power of God. The landscapes—or rather, universe-scapes—of *Paradise Lost* are vast, and described in the grandiloquent language that so impressed the young Pullman. The ongoing critical debate about *Paradise Lost*—whether it succeeds in its stated aim to "justify the ways of God to men" (*Paradise Lost*, Book 1, line 26), or rather depicts God and Christianity as essentially cruel, free will as a trap for mankind, and the human desire for knowledge as wrong—becomes a central theme to *His Dark Materials*. Yet Pullman's rewriting of the Bible and of *Paradise Lost* is consciously anti-God, and pro-temptation, with the Fall as "Completely essential [. . .] the best thing, the most important thing that ever happened to us" (see "Talking to Philip Pullman"). William Blake, the second of the writers acknowledged by Pullman, famously commented of *Paradise Lost* in his *The Marriage of Heaven and Hell* (1790) that "The reason Milton wrote in fetters when he wrote of angels and God, and at liberty when of devils and Hell, is because he was a true poet, and of the Devil's party without knowing it." Pullman takes on this comment, claiming himself to be knowingly of "the Devil's party" in his inversion of the morality of the Fall, and also in his exploration of the rich imaginative possibilities afforded by devils, Hell, and the multiple worlds traveled through by Satan and the angels in *Paradise Lost*.

Blake is acknowledged by Pullman not just for his comments upon Milton, but also for his own poetic vision, particularly in the *Songs of Innocence* (1789) and *Experience* (1794). These lyrics are one of the sources of Lyra's name, as she is "The Little Girl Lost" and "The Little Girl Found." But it is their confusion of the categories of innocence and experience, and their strange, disturbing and visionary landscapes, that Pullman has plundered most thoroughly for *Northern Lights*, *The Subtle Knife* and *The Amber Spyglass*.

The third acknowledgement that Pullman makes is to an essay by the nineteenth-century German writer, Heinrich von Kleist. "On the Marionette Theatre" (1810; sometimes translated as "The Puppet Theatre") tells of the encounter between the narrator and a dancer. Their discourse on the puppet theater, and their anecdotes of a young man coming to consciousness of his own grace, and so losing it, and of a fighting bear, nourishes Pullman's thematics in the trilogy, but also supplies the inspiration for one of its chief characters: Iorek Byrnison, the armored bear. Kleist's metaphors of the Fall distill in only a few thousands words the central concerns of Pullman's 1,300 page trilogy.

These three sources specifically named in *The Amber Spyglass* are of vital importance to the creation of the trilogy. Yet many more sources have gone into the making of *His Dark Materials*, for it is a deeply intertextual work. Pullman is indebted to folk and fairy tale, to Greek myth and Romantic poetry, to traditional tropes of children's literature and to the *Bildungsroman* (novel of growing up). He also borrows ideas from science and from the cinema, and even from the Helsinki phone book—the source of Serafina Pekkala's name—proving his own adage in the Acknowledgements to "'Read like a butterfly, write like a bee'" (AS, p. 549).

Through his intertextual ingenuity, Pullman has woven in *His Dark Materials* a new myth—as Andrew Marr put it in the *Daily Telegraph*, "Pullman does for atheism what C. S. Lewis did for God." In so doing he has won prizes for both child and adult books, and attracted large audiences, composed both of children and of adults. In various pronouncements about the divide between child and adult literature, and his own capacity to cross it, Pullman has proved himself both a controversialist and a powerful advocate of children's literature. In the acceptance speech he made on winning the Carnegie Medal for *Northern Lights*, for example, he made these comments, repeated on the Random House website:

There are some themes, some subjects, too large for adult fiction; they can only be dealt with adequately in a children's book.

The reason for that is that in adult literary fiction, stories are there on sufferance. Other things are felt to be more important: technique, style, literary knowingness. Adult writers who deal in straightforward stories find themselves sidelined into a genre such as crime or science fiction, where no one expects literary craftsmanship.

Pullman's emphatic assertion of the primacy of children's writing and its capacity to deal with the big themes of good and evil, innocence and experience, faith and morality, is entirely at one with his own achievement in *His Dark Materials*. The means by which this is accomplished is not through overt philosophizing, however, but through the vehicle of story. As Pullman went on to say in his speech, "stories are vital," the pre-eminent way both to entertain and to transmit morality and beliefs, and "the world we create." It is for this "vertiginous delight of storytelling," as Pullman described it (in "Talking to Philip Pullman") that his work has become so loved, acclaimed but also pilloried. For Pullman's power of story is a great one, stirring the hearts and minds of children and adults, advocates and opponents. The next chapter explores in more detail Pullman's achievement.

2

The Novels

Introduction

Three novels—*Northern Lights*, *The Subtle Knife* and *The Amber Spyglass*—make up *His Dark Materials*. The trilogy as a whole is a richly complex work, with a fast-paced plot featuring a wealth of characters, and interwoven with ideas of religion, science and philosophy. This chapter explores the plot, character and themes of *His Dark Materials*, as well as offering an interpretation of them. It divides into three main sections: "Adventure," "Politics" and "Story." "Adventure" introduces the characters and plots, and considers Pullman's imaginative creations and alternate worlds. "Politics" investigates the themes of the trilogy, including ideas of innocence and experience, religion and the Church, and environmentalism. The final section, "Story," is concerned both with Pullman's work as a writer, and the ways in which he incorporates storytelling as a central theme into his work.

Adventure

Worlds of adventure are opened up within *His Dark Materials*. The protagonists of the trilogy traverse multiple worlds, encountering friends and enemies in both human and other forms. From the beginning, *Northern Lights* conjures up a sense of these various worlds as, in a place called "Oxford," the reader is introduced to "Lyra and her dæmon" (*NL*, p. 3). These two are sneaking through the Hall toward the forbidden Retiring Room, and the great adventure on which, unknowingly, they are soon to embark.

With these opening words, a sense of familiarity and strangeness is induced. Lyra is immediately situated as the heroine of the adventure, already intruding into a place where she shouldn't be. In plot terms, Lyra is recognizable as an inquisitive, plucky heroine, familiar to readers of children's books. Yet Lyra is accompanied by a thing—her "dæmon"—that is unknown to the reader. As the first page continues, more information is given about this strange thing. It can talk, and tells Lyra to "'Behave yourself'" (*NL*, p. 3). It seems to have its own consciousness, or at least one that conflicts with Lyra's more impudent nature. Next, the reader is told of the name of this "dæmon"—Pantalaimon—and that its current form is that of a dark brown moth.

The Hall of the Oxford college into which the girl and her demon are venturing is an environment both real and fantastic, modeled closely on real-life Oxford colleges: places of ritual, tradition and, frequently, struggles for power. As the reader of *His Dark Materials* discovers, although Lyra grows up in a place called Oxford, there are significant differences between this "Oxford" and the "Oxford" in which Pullman studied and continues to live. Jordan College, for example, is an invention of Lyra's world. Lyra's Oxford, moreover, is to be found in a place called "Brytain" rather than Britain, a parallel place "like ours, but different in many ways," as Pullman puts it in a note that prefaces *Northern Lights*. This alternative reality is sharply indicated when Lyra ventures into the Oxford of Will's world, the world that is, as Pullman's note to *The Subtle Knife* phrases it, "the universe we know." She sees "people of every sort, women dressed like men, Africans, even a group of Tartars meekly following their leader, all neatly dressed and hung about with little black cases"—Japanese tourists, it may be assumed. She is amazed by her visit to the cinema, but is nearly caught out in "this mock-Oxford" by asking for a bar of "chocolatl," rather than chocolate (SK, p. 78).

Such a pattern of recognition and defamiliarization continues throughout the trilogy, with its introduction of strange characters and new worlds. The adventures that are to come for Lyra and Pantalaimon, and for Will and Iorek, and for Lord Asriel and Mrs. Coulter, oscillate between Pullman's rich invention and readers' recognition. This section, "Adventure," explores some of those inventions, particularly through the characters of the trilogy, and follows their incorporation into the world-traversing plots of *His Dark Materials*.

Dæmons

Pullman's invention of the "dæmon" is one of the most striking features of the trilogy, one that Pullman has described in various interviews as being one of the best ideas he ever had. It is fitting to start a consideration of the trilogy as a whole with them.

In Lyra's world, each human being has a constant companion in his or her dæmon, which takes the form of an animal. Over the opening chapters, certain rules and patterns begin to emerge about humans and their dæmons. A dæmon is nearly always the opposite sex to its human (though there are exceptions, including the gyptians' pastry-cook spy at Jordan, Bernie Johansen (NL, p. 125)). Adult's dæmons remain in one animal form, while children's dæmons change, as Pantalaimon's first appearance as a moth, but later in "sleeping-form as an ermine" indicates (NL, p. 28). Servants' dæmons are almost invariably dogs. Just as humans talk to and touch each other, so do their dæmons, but there is a "prohibition against human-dæmon contact [that] went so deep that even in battle no warrior would touch an enemy's dæmon" (*NL*, p. 143). A wound inflicted on either human or dæmon is felt by the other, and if humans die, so do their dæmons. For a human to be separated from his or her dæmon causes immense physical pain and mental anguish. Lyra feels it as "a strange tormenting feeling when your dæmon was pulling at the link between you; part physical pain deep in the chest, part intense sadness and love" (*NL*, p. 194).

When Lyra meets the second protagonist of the trilogy, Will, in *The Subtle Knife*, each is equally surprised. Will, who comes from a world of no dæmons, finds Pantalaimon's shape-shifting "extraordinary" (*SK*, p. 21). Lyra, on the other hand, is shocked to find a properly living person with no visible dæmon: she resorts to thinking that Will's dæmon must be inside him. Lyra's dual nature—human and dæmon—is apparent in her attempt to explain to Will what he is lacking, an explanation that makes Will feel "profoundly alone":

'Me and Pantalaimon. Us. Your dæmon en't *separate* from you. It's you. You're part of each other. En't there *anyone* in your world like us? Are they all like you, with their dæmons all hidden away?" (*SK*, p. 26)

Eventually, Will, too, will discover his dæmon, Kirjava. Dæmons, then, are much more than a companion. Rather, they are intrinsically part of their human, though taking on a separate physical form. As such they reflect the character of their human, but also, as with the opening scenes of *Northern Lights*, can act as a restraint, setting up an externalised internal dialogue. When Lyra and Pan see the Master of the College put poison in wine destined for her uncle, Lord Asriel, they argue about what to do. Pan advocates minding their own business. Lyra disagrees completely, stating that they don't have "any choice," and are now involved in the murder plot (*NL*, p. 9). At this point she goads Pan with words that suggest one possible explanation for the concept of the dæmon. She says, "'You're supposed to know about conscience, aren't you?'" (*NL*, p. 9). The dæmon could be seen as an expression of a human's conscience. Yet, as Lyra's thoughts go on to reveal, it is she that is the moral being in the dual relationship at this point, and she who has to make increasingly difficult decisions as they both set off on their adventures through multiple worlds:

Lyra felt a mixture of thoughts contending in her head, and she would have liked nothing better than to share them with her dæmon, but she was proud too. Perhaps she should try to clear them up without his help. (*NL*, p. 9)

It is clear, then, that human and dæmon, although physically and emotionally linked, do not share the same consciousness, and it is the human who is the controlling party in the relationship.

Other beings from Lyra's world have different relationships to their dæmons, or like the humans from Will's world, do not have dæmons at all. The witches have dæmons, but can be separated by a much greater physical distance than a human could withstand. The armored bears of the North do not have dæmons, but rather, as Lyra's accomplice Iorek Byrnison explains it, "'A bear's armour is his soul, just as your dæmon is your soul'" (*NL*, p. 196).

Iorek's explanation of his armor as his "soul" provides another theory for what the dæmon is: a personification (or rather, an animalification) of the soul. Yet the division between human and dæmon is certainly not one of body and soul, as both have a physical form and their own consciousness. Marina Warner, in the epilogue to *Fantastic Metamorphoses, Other Worlds: Ways of Telling the Self*, sees Pullman's invention as a direct response to the closing words of Plato's *Republic*, written over two thousand years earlier. The souls of dead Homeric heroes take on a new incarnation, in the form of a demon. Warner interprets Pullman's trilogy as developing "the relation between metamorphosis as truth-telling about people, through an extraordinary dramatic device, a personal dæmon accompanying every character, a kind of external soul."

Yet dæmons do not function in *His Dark Materials* solely as a philosophical idea, nor as an attractively rich creation whose appeal to children will draw on their own frequently invented imaginary friends—constant and controllable companions. Pullman has described that he did not want dæmons to be "a picturesque detail," but to be fully integrated into the themes and plotting of the trilogy. As he goes on to explain, dæmons "symbolise the difference between the infinite plasticity, the infinite potentiality and mutability of childhood and the fixed nature of adulthood" ("An Introduction to . . . Philip Pullman"). This relates to the "settling" of dæmons as children pass through adolescence into adulthood. In a key passage in *Northern Lights*, Lyra discusses this with the Able-Seaman during her voyage to the North:

"Why do dæmons have to settle?" Lyra said. "I want Pantalaimon to be able to change for ever. So does he."

"Ah, they always have settled, and they always will. That's part of growing up. There'll come a time when you'll be tired of his changing about, and you'll want a settled kind of form for him."

"I never will!"

"Oh, you will. You'll want to grow up like all the other girls. Anyway, there's compensations for a settled form."

"What are they?"

"Knowing what kind of person you are. Take old Belisaria. She's a seagull, and that means I'm a kind of seagull too. I'm not grand and splendid and beautiful, but I'm a tough old thing and I can survive anywhere and always find a bit of food and company. That's worth knowing, that is. And when your dæmon settles, you'll know the sort of person you are." (NL, p. 167)

Dæmons are intimately connected to the process of character development, the journey from innocence to experience, and questions of choice and morality. The General Oblation Board's project to sever children from their dæmons in the Experimental Station in Bolvangar before the settling—and oncoming sexual maturity—of adolescence is then linked to *His Dark Materials*' rewriting of the story of Adam and Eve and the Fall, as the "Politics" section of this chapter explores. Lyra—the protagonist of *His Dark Materials*—will find herself inextricably caught up in these plot developments.

Lyra

In *The Amber Spyglass*, as Lyra walks through the land of the dead, the Chevalier Tialys looks down, to see all the dead following "that bright and living spark Lyra Silvertongue" (AS, p. 318). The gloom of the underworld accentuates Lyra as one of the most vivid heroines of children's literature.

Lyra Belacqua—as she is called before her friend Iorek dubs her Silvertongue—spent her early years in Oxford. She is left in the care of the Master and Scholars of Jordan College to live a "half-wild" life among its "grandeur and ritual" (NL, p. 37). Like many of the protagonists of children's books, she is an orphan, the child of the Count and Countess Belacqua who were, she has been told, killed in an accident in the North. Her uncle, Lord Asriel, leaves her upbringing to the Master and Scholars. Lyra's early education is haphazard, led by the Scholars' interests and hampered by her own "fidgeting" nature (NL, p. 32). Much of her childhood is spent in other parts of Oxford, however: on the roofs and in the cellars of the colleges with her good friend Roger the kitchen boy; in the streets of Oxford, fighting pitched battles with the children of other colleges and the "townies"; and in the rougher districts of Jericho, among the brick-burners' children and the gyptians (*NL*, p. 36). Despite her aristocratic lineage, Lyra's unusual guardians do not prevent her excursions into the outside world, thus allowing her friendships to cross class boundaries. Lyra revels in the "rich seething stew of alliances and enmities and feuds and treaties which was a child's life in Oxford" (*NL*, p. 36), and is described as "a coarse and greedy little savage" (*NL*, p. 37), a "barbarian" (*NL*, p. 35).

Yet Lyra realizes that her childhood Oxford is not all there is, and that "somewhere in her life there was a connection with the high world of politics represented by Lord Asriel" (*NL*, p. 37). It is this connection that *His Dark Materials* chronicles, as Lyra is swept into danger, intrigue, and betrayal. In the course of the plot, it is revealed that Lyra is not, after all, an orphan, but the child of the great adversaries and former lovers Lord Asriel and Mrs. Coulter, entrusted as a baby to the care of the gyptian Ma Costa and then to Jordan College. Lord Asriel and Mrs. Coulter offer no parental safety for Lyra, and their treachery and occasional alliances force Lyra to rely on her own capacity for friendship.

Lyra has a great destiny within the stories that unfold in *His Dark Materials*, which is whispered and hinted throughout the three volumes. The first intimation of her role is spoken by the Master of Jordan College. She has a "'major'" part to play, and will commit a "'great betrayal,'" but "'must do it all without realizing what she's doing'" (*NL*, pp. 32, 33, 32). The witches, according to their Consul, have spoken of this great destiny for centuries (*NL*, p. 175), and in *The Subtle Knife*, a captured witch is tortured in order to discover the nature of this destiny (*SK*, pp. 39–41). Yet Lyra is unaware of her destiny and is, according to Farder Coram the wise old gyptian, "'a strange, innocent creature'" (*NL*, p. 175). Her destiny as "'Eve! Mother of all! Eve, again! Mother Eve!'" (*SK*, p. 328) is explored in this chapter's section on "Politics."

As Lyra moves toward her destiny in *The Amber Spyglass*, her character is revealed as resourceful, brave and loyal. She can also, however, be haughty, self-righteous and is an inveterate liar. She makes deep alliances with Iorek, Will and Lee Scoresby, but also commits two great betrayals—firstly of her friend Roger at the end of *Northern Lights*, whom she unknowingly leads to his death at the hands of Lord Asriel, and then to the betrayal that the Master prophesies—of her own Pantalaimon, from whom she must separate on the riverbank in order to reach the land of the dead.

Iorek renames his friend Lyra Silvertongue for her storytelling talents. These prove vital in winning many of the battles of *His Dark Materials*, and particularly for extricating Lyra from difficult situations. Lyra helps Iorek win back the bear kingdom from Iofur Raknison, a bear who has erred from his nature by desiring a dæmon. Lyra convinces Iofur she is Iorek's dæmon, but willing to become his if he defeats Iorek in battle. Lyra realizes Iofur's weakness, and through her verbal skill sets a trap, and the fight that Iorek will eventually win. In situations of danger and uncertainty Lyra frequently lies, parading a series of alternate identities: Lizzie Brooks when she is captured and taken to the Experimental Station at Bolvangar; the child of a duke and duchess when she is on the banks of land of the dead; and "Alice" when a suspicious man in a top hat attempts to put brandy in her coffee when she runs away from Mrs. Coulter's London house. She lies for self-protection, but also, sometimes, for the sheer love of invention, as her narration of the false story of her duke and duchess parents demonstrates:

> "I'll tell you all about it," said Lyra.
> As she said that, as she took charge, part of her felt a little stream of pleasure rising upwards in her breast like the bubbles in champagne. And she knew Will was watching, and she was happy that he could see her doing what she was best at, doing it for him and for all of them. (*AS*, p. 276)

The morality of storytelling, and the lessons that Lyra learns in the land of the dead are examined in the "Story" section of this chapter. The control that Lyra feels when she has a captive audience to tell her stories to, though, is one similar to the feeling she has when reading the alethiometer. The alethiometer is a truth-telling device given to Lyra by the Master of Jordan College. She quickly learns how to read this golden compass by carefully watching the movements of its hands from symbol to symbol in response to her questions. The alethiometer becomes one of Lyra's principle weapons in the battle of *His Dark Materials*, inferring upon her the qualities of a seer, able to communicate with a consciousness that people of her own world name "Dust."

Lyra's relationship to the alethiometer, however, also signals a change in her own relationships, and a development of her character. When, in *The Subtle Knife*, she enters the parallel world of Will's Oxford, the compass tells her, *"You must concern yourself with the boy. Your task is to help him find his father. Put your mind to that."* (*SK*, p. 83) This Oxford is a place where Lyra is "a lost little girl in a strange world, belonging nowhere" (*SK*, p. 73). For a while, her quest becomes secondary to Will's, or at least can only be accomplished through following Will. In fact, from the second volume of the trilogy onward, after meeting Will, Lyra must unlearn some of her independence. This submission goes alongside Lyra's growing feelings for Will, as the two pass from childhood into adolescence. The softening of Lyra's character as the trilogy proceeds is an area of debate in *His Dark Materials*. *The Amber Spyglass* opens, for example, with Lyra imprisoned, fairy-tale-like, in a drugged sleep, waiting to be rescued by Will. This could be seen as a betrayal of Lyra's feminist credentials, as her mission becomes subservient to the male Will. Lyra must learn humility, dependence, trust and love, virtues that make her realize that, counter to her earlier wishes, she does want things to change, and to grow up. And yet, eventually, it is

Lyra's destiny as the new Eve that impels the plot of *His Dark Materials*, and Pullman's rewriting of this role makes a different feminist claim. The question that perhaps remains is whether the great sacrifice that Lyra and Will make at the end of the trilogy—to remain apart in their separate worlds—is once more one of denial, or instead an act of realism that will allow them to build the republic of heaven on earth.

Will

Will Parry is the second child protagonist in *His Dark Materials*, and yet he does not make an appearance until the second volume. *The Subtle Knife* opens with Will leading his frightened mother down the street, to leave her in the care of his piano teacher while he goes back home to search for a leather case of letters, and to discover more about the Arctic expedition during which his father, John Parry, disappeared many years earlier.

With an absent father and a mother troubled by the enemies in her own confused mind, Will is, like Lyra, a child cast adrift of adult supervision. He has to fend for himself, and face his responsibilities. When he returns home, he is woken in the night by men who have broken into the house, also looking for the case of letters. In the struggle that ensues, one of the men, tripped by Will's cat, falls down the stairs and is killed. The guilt that Will feels for this, and for the further violence he is drawn into when he meets Lyra, is one expression of his character, which is more reflective and thoughtful than Lyra's. In one scene, he "wrestled with the horror of what he'd done" (*SK*, p. 104). In another, when he kills for the second time, "His body revolted at what his instinct had made him do, and the result was a dry, sour, agonizing spell of kneeling and vomiting until his stomach and his heart were empty." (*AS*, p. 171) Will's revulsion is quite different from Lyra's blithe acceptance of Will as "*a murderer*," which the alethiometer tells her he is (*SK*, p. 29).

Pullman depicts the male child protagonist of *His Dark Materials*, therefore, as a more sensitive and troubled being than the female. He is quieter, more introspective, "good at not being noticed" (*SK*, p. 13), while Lyra likes nothing more than to be the center of attention. His difficult childhood, with his odd mother, means he also has knowledge of the cruelty of children, which he recognizes when he and Lyra are confronted by an angry mob of children in Cittàgazze (*SK*, pp. 237–42).

Nonetheless, Will proves himself to be a fierce and determined fighter, with the same bravery and loyalty displayed by Lyra. When he becomes the bearer of the "subtle knife," he also acquires a destiny, but one about which he is very equivocal. The knife has special powers: not only is it a weapon that can cut Iorek's armor like "butter" (*AS*, p. 112), but it can also open windows between the various worlds in *His Dark Materials*. Moreover, as the dying man that Will meets at the end of *The Subtle Knife* tells him, the bearer of the knife will have immense power in the "'greatest war there ever was'":

"We've had nothing but lies and propaganda and cruelty and deceit for all the thousands of years of human history. It's time we started again, but properly this time . . ."

He stopped to take in several rattling breaths.

"The knife," he went on after a minute; "they never knew what they were making, those old philosophers. They invented a device that could split open the very smallest particles of matter, and they used it to steal candy. They had no idea that they'd made the one weapon in all the universes that could defeat the tyrant. The Authority. God. The rebel angels fell because they didn't have anything like the knife; but now . . ." (*SK*, p. 334)

Will tries to refuse this weighty destiny, but by becoming the bearer of "Æsahættr," his nature as a "'warrior'" shows itself (*SK*, p. 335), and so he must accept his destiny by choosing to fight on the side of Lord Asriel. By choosing this path he must endure pain and suffering, but also, alongside Lyra, he will make powerful and redemptive choices that will change the universes of *His Dark Materials* forever.

The dying man at the end of *The Subtle Knife* that confronts Will with these choices is in fact his father, John Parry. During his Arctic expedition twelve years earlier, Parry and two companions go through a window between their world and another, but cannot find their way back. Parry investigates the multiplicity of worlds he then finds, and eventually, under the name of Dr. Stanislaus Grumman, becomes a member of the Berlin Academy in Lyra's world. It is his head that Lord Asriel pretends to show to the Master and Scholars of Jordan at the beginning of *Northern Lights*, although Grumman is in fact still alive and living as the shaman "Jopari" with a tribe of Siberian Tartars.

When Will eventually meets his father, the two only recognize their relationship seconds before John Parry dies, and at first it seems that Will is orphaned once again, and is left once more alone, but with an even greater knowledge of the task that lies before him. Yet due to his own, and Lyra's bravery, he will have another chance to encounter him in the land of the dead.

Lord Asriel

Lord Asriel first appears in the trilogy while Lyra is hidden in the Retiring Room. From the safety of a wardrobe, she observes the man she believes at this point in the story to be her uncle:

Lord Asriel was a tall man with powerful shoulders, a fierce dark face, and eyes that seemed to flash and glitter with savage laughter. It was a face to be dominated by, or to fight: never a face to patronize or pity. All his movements were large and perfectly balanced, like those of a wild animal, and when he appeared in a room like this, he seemed a wild animal held in a cage too small for it. (*NL*, p. 13)

Asriel is described as a Byronic hero, muscling with power and energy, and with a "savage," "wild" and dangerous edge. Elsewhere he is described as "'a passionate man'" (*NL*, p. 122). For Lyra, he is a figure of whom to be simultaneously proud and frightened, one whom, when she reveals herself, threatens to break her arm for her impudence in entering the Retiring Room. By recounting the plot to murder him, however, she saves Asriel's life, for which he begrudgingly allows her to watch and listen from the wardrobe to his explanation of his findings about Dust and the "Grumman expedition" in the North.

As Lyra eventually discovers, Asriel is not her uncle but her father. His love affair with the married Mrs. Coulter resulted in her birth, which Mrs. Coulter attempted to keep secret from her husband by hiding her away under the care of a gyptian woman. The vengeful husband attempted to kill Lyra, but Asriel arrived in time to save his child and kill the husband. In the resulting lawsuit, Asriel is not imprisoned, but all his vast wealth is confiscated.

Asriel is far from a loving father. When Lyra confronts him with her new knowledge of her parentage, his response is a dismissive, "'Yes. So what?'" (*NL*, p. 367). To him, family ties are secondary to his great utopian mission, a visionary project that requires the building of "'a bridge between this world and the world beyond the Aurora'"—the Northern Lights of the title of the first volume (*NL*, p. 188). That project is to create the republic of heaven. The "'free citizens'" of this republic, according to Asriel, will be released from the shackles imposed by the "'kingdom of heaven.'" It will be a world, as his ally Ogunwe puts it, with "'No kings, no bishops, no priests.'" (*AS*, p. 222). Asriel plans to bring to an end centuries of oppressive control by the Church and by its godhead—the "Authority." In *The Amber Spyglass*, he amasses a mighty army to achieve his aim. His passionate conviction of the physicality of the human body fuels his mission:

Lord Asriel turned and gripped his arm with fingers that all but bruised him to the bone.

"They haven't got *this!*" he said, and shook Ogunwe's arm violently. "They haven't got *flesh!*"

He laid his hand against his friend's rough cheek.

"Few as we are," he went on, "and short-lived as we are, and weak-sighted as we are—in comparison with them, we're still *stronger*. They *envy* us, Ogunwe! That's what fuels their hatred, I'm sure of it. They long to have our precious bodies, so solid and powerful, so well adapted to the good earth!" (*AS*, p. 394)

Asriel is, then, a leader of men but fighting for equality, and a fervent believer in the primacy of flesh. Yet his ambitions make him ruthless, as Lyra discovers at the end of *Northern Lights*. The alethiometer tells her that she has something to take to Asriel in order for him to accomplish his plan to bridge the worlds. She wrongly assumes that it is the alethiometer that he needs "'for this experiment'" (*NL*, p. 360). Her consequent arrival at Svalbard is greeted with horror by her father. Lyra has mistaken what it is she is bringing for him, because he needs a child for his experiment—a child who will be sacrificed in order for the Aurora to be torn apart. Until Asriel sees that Lyra is accompanied by another child, Roger, his shocked reaction shows that, despite his horror, he would consider using Lyra, his own child, for the experiment.

Asriel is estranged from Mrs. Coulter, but in erotically-charged moments at the end of *Northern Lights* which confuse the watching Lyra, he asks her to join him on his mission. Mrs. Coulter's refusal separates them for another two volumes, but they are reunited toward the end of *The Amber Spyglass*. Asriel's grand vision is not accomplished, and yet his dramatic fall into the abyss with Mrs. Coulter, as they unite to battle against the Authority's representative, Metatron, is their great sacrifice which allows Lyra to accomplish her destiny.

Mrs. Coulter

At the beginning of *Northern Lights*, all over Brytain, children are disappearing. One of these disappearances—or "bewitchings" (*NL*, p. 45)—introduces Mrs. Coulter. She is "a beautiful young lady" accompanied by a golden monkey dæmon (*NL*, p. 42). After tempting a group of children into a London cellar with promises of chocolatl, she tells them they are going on a voyage to the North. She offers to have letters delivered from the children to their families, but in a stroke of evil timing, she puts the children on the boat, "turned back inside [. . .] and threw the little bundle of letters into the furnace before leaving the way she had come" (*NL*, p. 45).

When Mrs. Coulter encounters Metatron, he delivers a scathing verdict on her life. He sees:

"Corruption and envy and lust for power. Cruelty and coldness. A vicious probing curiosity. Pure, poisonous, toxic malice. You have never from your earliest years shown a shred of compassion or sympathy or kindness without calculating how it would return to your advantage. You have tortured and killed without regret or hesitation; you have betrayed and intrigued and gloried in your treachery. You are a cess-pit of moral filth." (*AS*, p. 419)

This litany of accusation shakes her self-assurance, and yet she still manages to turn the situation to her advantage, using her own knowledge of human—and angel—sexuality to ensnare Metatron by persuading him of her capacity to do the same to Lord Asriel. Her behavior is equally treacherous toward her lover Lord Boreal, whom she kills.

Mrs. Coulter, then, is a seducer of both children and of men, an archetype of a certain kind of dangerous yet glamorous femininity. She comes to claim Lyra from Jordan when Lord Asriel is held captive by the armored bears in the North, and cannot protest. To Lyra,

Mrs. Coulter represents a new kind of womanhood that her early life in Jordan has not prepared her for, "one with dangerous powers and qualities such as elegance, charm, and grace" (*NL*, p. 82). Pantalaimon is uncertain about Mrs. Coulter, despite being as fascinated by her as Lyra is. When Mrs. Coulter washes Lyra's hair, Pantalaimon watches:

> with powerful curiosity until Mrs. Coulter looked at him, and he knew what she meant and turned away, averting his eyes modestly from these feminine mysteries as the golden monkey was doing. He had never had to look away from Lyra before. (*NL*, p. 78)

The division that "feminine mysteries" enforce between Lyra and her dæmon are a development of the disagreements the two have in the opening scenes, but also foretells the great separation that they will undergo in *The Amber Spyglass*. Yet before that parting, Lyra learns of another process of separation that Mrs. Coulter is involved with in her work as the head of the "General Oblation Board," or the "Gobblers," as the children call it. Rumors are rife about the work of the General Oblation Board, and Lyra, with her own capacity for storytelling and duplicity, tricks Lord Boreal into telling her more about it. What she and Pan learn about Mrs. Coulter's work precipitates their flight from her house.

When Lyra and Mrs. Coulter meet again at the Experimental Station in Bolvangar, Lyra is to learn much more about the terrifying process of "severing" or "intercision," in which captured children are forcibly separated from their dæmons with a silver guillotine. Mrs. Coulter surrounds herself with a bodyguard of adults who have undergone the same process. More will be said about the process itself, and its implications for Dust and for notions of sexuality, in the "Politics" section of this chapter. The rationale for Mrs. Coulter's involvement with the General Oblation Board, however, is defined by Lord Asriel as a result of her lust for power and her gender. He explains to Lyra:

"You see, your mother's always been ambitious for power. At first she tried to get it in the normal way, through marriage, but that didn't work, as I think you've heard. So she had to turn to the Church. Naturally she couldn't take the route a man could have taken—priesthood and so on—it had to be unorthodox; she had to set up her own order, her own channels of influence, and work through that. It was a good move to specialize in Dust. Everyone was frightened of it; no one knew what to do; and when she offered to direct an investigation, the Magisterium was so relieved that they backed her with money and resources of all kinds." (NL, p. 374)

Mrs. Coulter's manipulation, ingenuity and independence mark her similarities to her daughter, as Will realizes when, despite their enmity, "He found himself liking her, because she was brave, and because she seemed like a more complicated and richer and deeper Lyra" (AS, p. 150).

From her characteristics, Mrs. Coulter would seem to be as ill-fitted to be a mother-figure as Lord Asriel is to his fatherhood. Indeed, Lyra's very early years are overseen by the maternal Ma Costa, who is a very different model of womanhood. For the sake of power, Mrs. Coulter seems prepared, like Asriel, to kill her own daughter in order to prevent her destiny as a new Eve. Yet when she captures Lyra, and holds her prisoner in a cave at the beginning of *The Amber Spyglass*, she undergoes an unexpected transformation, and begins to have maternal feelings toward her daughter, wishing to protect her from the Magisterium, who want her killed. However, it is a difficult and sometimes dubious path to motherhood—she shields Lyra from the dangers of the world by keeping her drugged and imprisoned. Her subsequent motivations in *The Amber Spyglass*, when she joins Asriel's forces, are also suspicious. Her justification of her switch from the Church to the fighters for the republic of heaven is met with skepticism by Asriel himself, who sees her as "shameless" and lying "in the very marrow of her bones" (AS, p. 218). It is only later, when she treacherously leads Metatron to Asriel, that he accepts her love for Lyra, a love that she does not herself understand, a love which, as she says, "'came to me like a thief in the night'" (AS, pp. 426–7). The ultimate vindication of Mrs. Coulter is not in her words, however, but in her final action alongside Asriel in the battle with Metatron. As Asriel calls out to her, she makes the ultimate sacrifice:

The cry was torn from Lord Asriel, and with the snow leopard beside her, with a roaring in her ears, Lyra's mother stood and found her footing and leapt with all her heart, to hurl herself against the angel and her dæmon and her dying lover, and seize those beating wings, and bear them all down together into the abyss. (AS, p. 430)

Mary Malone

Mary Malone appears in many fewer scenes than Lyra, Will, Asriel and Mrs. Coulter in *His Dark Materials*, and yet her role is pivotal. She is a scientist based in a research laboratory, the "Dark Matter Research Unit," in Will's Oxford (SK, p. 87). The experiments she has been conducting are into what she calls "'Shadows,'" and describes as "'particles of consciousness'"—the Dust of Lyra's world (SK, p. 92). When Lyra reaches her, prompted by the alethiometer, her lab is about to be closed down, and so the appearance of an unusual young girl is greeted by Mary with more attention than it might otherwise have done.

The intervention made by Lyra into Mary's life leads her on a voyage through "the multiple worlds predicted by quantum theory" (AS, p. 90), to play anthropologist to the mulefas, a strange group of wheeled beasts, to discover the purpose of Dust, which she sights through her invention of the amber spyglass, and to fulfill her part in Lyra's destiny. Although she does not know what form this role will take, Dust, through her computer—the "Cave"—orders her to "Find the girl and the boy. Waste no more time. You must play the serpent." (*SK*, p. 261) Thus, Mary is cast in the role of the tempter to Lyra's Eve.

Before Mary can tempt Lyra, however, she must learn the lesson that Lyra teaches to the dead. The mulefas take her to the place where the dead, thanks to Lyra, escape the darkness of the land of the dead. One of the joyful dead speaks to Mary, telling her of the "injunction to *tell them stories*" (*AS*, p. 456). The phrase plays in Mary's mind, and the following chapter of *The Amber Spyglass*, "Marzipan," sees her carrying out its bidding.

The story that Mary tells in "Marzipan" is in response to Lyra's question about why she stopped being a nun. The story is to do with her loss of faith, but more importantly, reveals her experiences of sex and love, first as twelve-year-old at a party, and later, with an Italian man she meets during a scientific conference in Portugal. Mary's portrayal of her adolescent kisses, and her renunciation of the Church on a balmy summer night, opens Lyra's eyes, and excites her consciousness:

She felt a stirring at the roots of her hair: she found herself breathing faster. She had never been on a roller-coaster, or anything like one, but if she had, she would have recognized the sensations in her breast: they were exciting and frightening at the same time, and she had not the slightest idea why. The sensation continued, and deepened, and changed, as more parts of her body found themselves affected too. She felt as if she had been handed the key to a great house she hadn't known was there, a house that was somehow inside here, and as she turned the key, deep in the darkness of the building she felt other doors opening too, and lights coming on. She sat trembling, hugging her knees, hardly daring to breathe. (*AS*, pp. 467–8)

Lyra's nascent feelings for Will and her adolescent sexuality, culminate in a scene in a "little wood of silver-barked trees," where Lyra offers, and Will takes, the fruit that Mary packed for them earlier (*AS*, p. 489).

Friends, Allies, Enemies

In their journeys through the multiple worlds of *His Dark Materials*, Lyra, Will, Lord Asriel, Mrs. Coulter and Mary Malone encounter a vast range of other characters and creatures. Some of these become friends and allies: notably Iorek Byrnison, the armored bear; Lee Scoresby, the Texan aëronaut and Iorek's comrade-in-arms; the gyptians, including Farder Coram, John Faa and Ma Costa; and the witch Serafina Pekkala. Others are enemies, or at very least present challenges to the protagonists: the harpies of the land of the dead; the cliff-ghasts; and the clerics of the Magisterium, including the menacing figure of Father Gomez, the eager young priest detailed to follow Mary Malone and then to kill Lyra before she has a chance to fulfill her destiny. Some of these characters are human in form, others draw on traditional figures—angels, witches—and some, like the mulefas, are original in their creation. The teeming populations of *His Dark Materials* are nowhere more fully displayed than in the two opposing forces in *The Amber Spyglass*. On Lord Asriel's side are the Africans led by King Ogunwe; the Gallivespians, Chevalier Tialys and the Lady Salmakia, and their dragonfly steeds; and the rebel angels, including Balthamos and Baruch. On the side of the Magisterium and the Consistorial Court is the Swiss Guard; some of the witch clans; and the angels of the Authority, headed by Metatron. Both sides utilize a wealth of inventions in their struggle for supremacy, which in their inventiveness ally Pullman's trilogy to science fiction writing: the alethiometers (held both by Lyra and the

Magisterium); a demonic clockwork bug unleashed by Mrs. Coulter; the "intention craft" that is controlled by the processes of the mind alone; and the lodestone resonator, which the Gallivespians use to communicate with one another.

Multiple Worlds

All these characters, their armory and gadgetry, indicate the rich creativity of *His Dark Materials* and its fully conceived universes. Yet in the creation of multiple worlds Pullman attempts to do more than provide the canvas against which Lyra and Will's epic adventures are set. In his lecture "Let's Write It in Red," Pullman discusses the scientific notion of "phase space," which provides a prevailing metaphor for the trilogy. As he explains it:

phase space is a term from dynamics, and it refers to the untrackable complexity of changing systems. It's the notional space which contains not just the actual consequences of the present moment, but all the possible consequences.

Pullman illustrates this by quoting the poem "The Road Not Taken" (1916) by Robert Frost:

> Two roads diverged in a wood, and I—
> I took the one less travelled by,
> And that has made all the difference.

The multiple universes of *His Dark Materials* are drawn, then, to demonstrate this scientific principle as a literary metaphor, and also as a description of the process of writing itself. As Pullman elaborates, "I am surely not the only writer who has the distinct sense that every sentence I write is surrounded by the ghosts of the sentences I could have written at that point, but didn't." Yet Pullman's use of the concept of "phase space" is neither solely an illustration of a scientific principle, nor a metaphor for the process of creating a story, but also a means by which to articulate the necessity of choice. At the beginning of *The Amber Spyglass*, Will finds himself desolate. The witches he was traveling with at the end of *The Subtle Knife* are slain, Lyra and Serafina Pekkala are missing, and his only companions are the invisible and to Will, incomprehensible, angels Balthamos and Baruch:

Will considered what to do. When you choose one way out of many, all the ways you don't take are snuffed out like candles, as if they'd never existed. At the moment all Will's choices existed at once. But to keep them all in existence meant doing nothing. He had to choose, after all. (AS, pp. 14–5)

The insistence on Will's choice constitutes a form of morality at this point in the story. Will chooses to go on—to rescue Lyra, and then the dead, and also to join forces with Asriel. The future of the armored bears, with Iorek and Iofur battling for their leadership in *Northern Lights* is similarly discussed, with "two kinds of beardom opposed here, two futures, two destinies. Iofur had begun to take them in one direction, and Iorek would take them in another, and in the same moment, one future would close forever as the other began to unfold." (NL, pp. 349–50) The final settling of a child's dæmon as he or she reaches adulthood is another example of this: character is constituted by the choices made earlier on, and the rejection of other paths. Phase space then becomes a politicized metaphor, one in which choices are indicative of morality. The agonizing choice that Lyra and Will are forced to make at the end of the trilogy—whether to see each other occasionally but close the window through which the dead escape, or whether to say goodbye for all time—is the greatest example of the principle Pullman incorporates into *His Dark Materials*. When Lyra and Will decide they must stay apart forever, they make one promise, at Lyra's suggestion:

"What I thought was that if you—maybe just once a year—if we could come here at the same time, just for an hour or something, then we could pretend we were close again—because we *would* be close, if you sat here and I sat just *here* in my world." (AS, p. 537)

The two Oxfords are laid over one another as a palimpsest, and the bench in the Botanic Garden in Oxford is the symbol of their choice, a heartrending image of the two young lovers' sacrifice, of all they have given up for the sake of saving their universes.

Politics

The worlds of adventure traversed by Lyra and Will are not, as the politicized metaphor of phase space suggests, merely the highly illustrated backdrop for one of the most richly inventive narratives of recent literary history. *His Dark Materials* is also a very political trilogy, which is apparent from the opening pages, as Lyra invades the male space of Jordan College's Retiring Room, and discovers the treachery and power games of the adult world. Through the intensely fought battlefields of the trilogy, Pullman develops the overarching themes of *His Dark Materials*: innocence, experience and sexuality; religion and the Church; and environmentalism. It is these political themes that this section of the chapter investigates, via Pullman's invention of Dust and dæmons, and his rewriting of "*Paradise Lost* for teenagers."

Innocence and Experience

Another rewriting occurs at the end of *Northern Lights*, as Lord Asriel explains to Lyra about Dust. The Bible is itself the text upon which *Paradise Lost* is based—Eve's temptation, and Adam and Eve's consequent banishment from the garden in Genesis. Lord Asriel reads to Lyra from Pullman's subtly altered version, changing the tempter's words to "*'For God doth know that in the day ye eat thereof, then your eyes shall be opened, and your dæmons shall assume their true forms, and ye shall be as gods, knowing good and evil.'*" (NL, p. 372) The consequences of Adam and Eve eating the forbidden tree's fruit are extreme:

"And the eyes of them both were opened, and they saw the true form of their dæmons, and spoke with them.

"But when the man and the woman knew their own dæmons, they knew that a great change had come upon them, for until that moment it had seemed that they were at one with all the creatures of the earth and the air, and there was no difference between them:

"And they saw the difference, and they knew good and evil; and they were ashamed, and they sewed fig leaves together to cover their nakedness . . ." (NL, p. 372)

For the Church, this Fall is the source of "original sin" (NL, p. 371), of the transition of innocence to experience, and also, in Pullman's version, of the fixing of the dæmon in its "*'true form.'*" The recent scientific discoveries in Lyra's world provide "'a physical proof that something happened when innocence changed into experience'" (NL, p. 373). Rusakov, a Russian scientist, discovered what Asriel terms "'a new kind of elementary particle'" which clusters around human beings, and particularly adults (NL, p. 370). Through reference to another biblical passage, the elementary particles come to be called "Dust" (NL, p. 373): "*In the sweat of thy face shalt thou eat bread, till thou return unto the ground; for out of it wast thou taken: for dust thou art, and unto dust shalt thou return . . ."* (NL, p. 373).

Mrs. Coulter's route to power was "'to specialize in Dust,'" directing an investigation into it on behalf of the Church. The horrors of the General Oblation Board, then, are directly connected to Pullman's themes of innocence and experience, his concentration on religion and the Church, and his rewriting of *Paradise Lost*.

Mrs. Coulter's work at the Experimental Station in Bolvangar, in which the children she has bewitched away from their homes are forcibly separated from their dæmons, is concerned with the transition from innocence to experience a child makes when passing through adolescence to adulthood. Dust, as the "'physical proof'" of this transition, is closely connected to the process the children undergo at the Experimental Station, rumors of which circulate the North. Dr. Lanselius, the witches' consul, says to Lyra and the gyptians that he has "'heard the phrase *the Maystadt Process*,'" and also "'*intercision*,'" in connection to the General Oblation Board's mission (*NL*, p. 171). Lyra, however, discovers the terrible truth of these euphemisms. She meets her old friend Tony Makarios, who has undergone the process and lives a half-life without his dæmon, and then, when she is captured, she discovers glass cases full of dæmons that have been severed from human children. When she is discovered spying on the scientists at the Station, she almost undergoes severing herself. She is forced into a separate compartment of a mesh cage from Pantalaimon, and the silver blade of the guillotine is already descending when Mrs. Coulter arrives, and saves them. This, incidentally, is the first moment when Mrs. Coulter seems to show some maternal feeling for Lyra—she is "in a moment haggard and horror-struck" (*NL*, p. 279).

Later, Mrs. Coulter recovers from her shock to justify the severing process to Lyra:

"All that happens is a little cut, and then everything's peaceful. For ever! You see, your dæmon's a wonderful friend and companion when you're young, but at the age we call puberty, the age you're coming to very soon, darling, dæmons bring all sort of troublesome thoughts and feelings, and that's what lets Dust in. A quick little operation before that, and you're never troubled again. And your dæmon stays with you, only . . . just not connected. Like a . . . like a wonderful pet, if you like. The best pet in the world! Wouldn't you like that?" (*NL*, pp. 284–5)

Lyra is repelled by Mrs. Coulter's disingenuous explanation of the work of the Oblation Board, though for the time being she keeps her thoughts to herself, and waits for her moment to free the children from the Station. Lyra escapes a future as a severed adult, like the nurses in the Station with "their strange blank incuriosity, the way their little trotting dæmons seemed to be sleepwalking" (*NL*, p. 284).

Mrs. Coulter's repudiation of Dust as "'something bad, something wrong, something evil and wicked'" (*NL*, p. 284), is part of her attempt to win Lyra over through her mention of the "'troublesome thoughts and feelings'" that begin to occur at puberty. Sexuality and Dust are connected, and it is the Church's fear of and distaste for the onset of sexual maturity that legitimates Mrs. Coulter's experiments. As Lord Asriel later explains to Lyra, this fear and distaste extends back to the founding story of Adam and Eve's Fall, through Eve's desire for knowledge and to be, as the serpent says, "'*as gods, knowing good and evil.*'" Yet Mrs. Coulter's motives in leading the Church's investigations into Dust—as with many of her actions— are profoundly dubious: she is a very sexual being, and repeatedly uses her powers of seduction to achieve her own ends.

This paradox is one of many in *His Dark Materials*, in which dualistic thoughts—of the opposition between innocence and experience, between good and evil, are contested by Pullman, as William Blake did before him. Mary's explanation of good and evil gives a truer representation of Pullman's belief in the combination of opposites:

"When you stopped believing in God," [Will] went on, "did you stop believing in good and evil?"

"No. But I stopped believing there was a power of good and a power of
evil that were outside us. And I came to believe that good and evil are names
for what people do, not for what they are. All we can say is that this is a good
deed, because it helps someone, or that's an evil one, because it hurts them.
People are too complicated to have simple labels." (*AS*, pp. 470–1)

Mary's loss of faith—but not of morality—is an indication of the attitudes toward religion that *His Dark Materials* conveys, and that
Pullman's rewriting of the myth of Adam and Eve promotes.

The Fall

Lyra's escape from being severed is one that will eventually lead her
to achieve her destiny as the new Eve. It is here that *His Dark Materials* demonstrates its grand project of rewriting *Paradise Lost* and its
narrative of the Fall, which Pullman views, as the first chapter of
this guide mentioned, as both essential and positive: a reversal of the
traditional morality associated with the story.

In *His Dark Materials*, there are three versions of the story of the
Fall. The first is the one that Asriel reads to Lyra from the Bible, a
version closely adapted from the real-world Old Testament of Juda-
ism and Christianity. The second is a story narrated to Mary Malone
by the mulefas. In this story, the mulefas gain knowledge—"*memory
and wakefulness*"—through their use of the seed-pods, and creation
of "sraf," as the mulefas term Dust (*AS*, p. 236). The relationship of
happy mutuality between the mulefas and the seed-pod trees is a
very different one from the harsh banishment of Adam and Eve by
God. When Mary meets the mulefas, however, this symbiotic relationship is in jeopardy: the seed-pod trees are dying, and Dust—as
Mary discovers by looking through the amber spyglass—is drifting

out to sea rather than falling on the trees and fertilizing them. Her understanding of Dust leads her toward her own role as tempter in the third version of the story of the Fall, in which Lyra plays Eve, and Will is Adam.

Mary's narration of her sexual experiences is the spur to Lyra fulfilling her destiny as Eve. Her growing feelings for Will become apparent to her as she listens to Mary's story. On the morning in which Lyra and Will set off to find their dæmons, they walk together as if they were "the only people in the world" (AS, p. 483). Their pursuit of their dæmons leads them into the "little wood of silver-barked trees," to their declaration of their love for one another, and to a physical manifestation of that love. For Father Gomez, commissioned by the Church to follow and stop them, although he is stopped himself by Balthamos, their adolescent sexuality is "mortal sin" (AS, p. 489), but for Lyra and Will it is a mixture of confusion and happiness and adoration. Pullman's third version of the Fall is a celebration of adolescent sexuality, and a vindication of a very different morality to that espoused by the Church: the Church of *His Dark Materials*, but also the real-world Christian church, and its tortured and frequently repressive stance toward sex.

The implications of Lyra and Will's venture into the wood, and adulthood, is observed, and welcomed, by Mary and the mulefas. The drift of Dust is reversed, and the seed-pod trees once more are "drinking in this golden rain" after being "starved for so long" (AS, p. 496). Mary sees Lyra and Will returning to the mulefa village:

There was no need for the glass; she knew what she would see; they would seem to be made of living gold. They would seem the true image of what human beings always could be, once they had come into their inheritance.

The Dust pouring down from the stars had found a living home again, and these children-no-longer-children, saturated with love, were the cause of it all. (AS, p. 497)

Lyra and Will's transition, then, from children to young adults, is portrayed with extreme favor, and their intervention in the history of Dust is crucial in the reorienting of morality in Pullman's revision of the Fall.

Religion and the Church

The vision of young love and a new moral order at the end of *The Amber Spyglass* is in contradiction to the morality of the Church in *His Dark Materials*. The Church of Lyra's world is recognizably based on the Christianity of the real world—the founding story of Adam and Eve is one example. Yet, like many things in Lyra's world, there are differences too. As the early sections of *Northern Lights* describing Jordan College reveal, the Chapel is filled with "philosophical apparatus," and the College is a pre-eminent "centre of experimental theology" (*NL*, p. 35). The Church of Lyra's world is run by the "Magisterium," under which various branches jostle for supremacy: the Consistorial Court of Discipline, the Society of the Work of the Holy Spirit, the General Oblation Board.

It is the Consistorial Court that commissions Father Gomez, a figure "pale and trembling with zealotry" (*AS*, p. 73), to track down Lyra and kill her before she is tempted. The President's justification for this murderous act is to prevent Lyra's destiny as a new Eve. The fundamentalist Consistorial Court would also accept its own destruction for the sake of destroying Dust, which they see as at the root of all evil:

"If in order to destroy Dust we also have to destroy the Oblation Board, the College of Bishops, every single agency by which the Holy Church does the work of the Authority—then so be it. It may be, gentlemen, that the Holy Church itself was brought into being to perform this very task and to perish in the doing of it. But better a world with no church and no Dust than a world where every day we have to struggle under the hideous burden of sin. Better a world purged of all that!" (*AS*, p. 74)

The President's avowal has a destructive, skewed logic that would prefer nothingness to an existence with "'the hideous burden of sin.'" This is an extreme denial, and an image is built up of the Church as populated with life-denying clerics, whose lust for power is only eclipsed by their fervent desire to eradicate Dust—and its correlatives of human knowledge and sexuality—from the world. Father MacPhail, the President, personifies the Church in his ascetic lifestyle:

He was a dark-featured man, tall and imposing, with a shock of wiry grey hair, and he would have been fat were it not for the brutal discipline he imposed on his body: he drank only water and ate only bread and fruit, and he exercised for an hour daily under the supervision of a trainer of champion athletes. As a result, he was gaunt and lined and restless. His dæmon was a lizard. (*AS*, p. 73)

The Church and its leaders are set against the life-affirming qualities of the heroes of *His Dark Materials,* and above all against Lyra and Will's adolescent love. In the plot of the trilogy, however, it is Lord Asriel's forces who array themselves against the Church and the powers of the Magisterium. Asriel's attitudes toward Dust and the Church are, nonetheless, complex. After her conversation with him at the end of *Northern Lights,* Lyra is left confused. Asriel explains his paradoxical mission to her:

"Somewhere out there is the origin of all the Dust, all the death, the sin, the misery, the destructiveness in the world. Human beings can't see anything without wanting to destroy it, Lyra. *That's* original sin. And I'm going to destroy it. Death is going to die." (*NL*, p. 377)

Asriel equates Dust with death, sin, misery and destructiveness, and thus wants to kill Death. After Asriel crosses to the next world in pursuit of his mission, Lyra debates with Pan whether Dust is a good or a bad thing. Pan says that Asriel is "'going to find the source of Dust and destroy it'" (*NL*, p. 397), whereas in fact he says he will destroy *death*. The purpose of Dust remains unconfirmed until the final volume of the trilogy, by which time Asriel's mission has solidified into a whole scale war against the forces of the Church. The witch Ruta Skadi reports on her conversations with Asriel about his forthcoming battle against the Authority:

"He showed me that to rebel was right and just, when you considered what the agents of the Authority did in his name . . . And I thought of the Bolvangar children, and the other terrible mutilations I have seen in our own south-lands; and he told me of many more hideous cruelties dealt out in the Authority's name—of how they capture witches, in some worlds, and burn them alive, sisters, yes, witches like ourselves . . .

"He opened my eyes. He showed me things I never had seen, cruelties and horrors all committed in the name of the Authority, all designed to destroy the joys and the truthfulness of life." (*SK*, p. 283)

Asriel's passionate campaign against the crimes committed in the name of the Authority convinces Ruta Skadi and the other witches to join his forces. Asriel makes it his mission not just to battle against the forces of the Church, but against the Authority himself. As his servant Thorold reports, Asriel is attempting a second rebellion against the Authority, after the failure of the rebel angels that is told in *Paradise Lost*. Asriel's mission, then, is to institute a republic of heaven. When the Authority eventually appears in *The Amber Spyglass*, he proves a poor comparison to the dynamic Asriel: he is old, and terrified, "crying like a baby and cowering away into the lowest corner," "demented and powerless" (*AS*, p. 431). This depiction of the Authority would prove contentious to Christian critics of the trilogy. Likewise, Pullman has been criticized for stereotyping the

Church clerics, and for disrespectfully portraying the Christian God, as Chapter Three explores. Others, however, have applauded Pullman's alternate morality, free of organized religion but deeply rooted in choice and individual responsibility.

Environmentalism

In the mulefas' world, Dust is drifting out to sea, the seed-pod trees are dying, and the mutually interdependent relationship of the trees and the mulefas is unraveling. The mulefas tell Mary of the many years of living with their trees "in perpetual joy" (AS, p. 139). Their communion with nature is symbiotic, and their lifestyle almost hippy-like in its gentle but enriching existence. The threat posed to this lifestyle is from the disruptions caused to the boundaries between the worlds 300 years earlier, when the subtle knife was invented and used to make windows from one world to the next. The mulefas, and their close relationship to the land, are a fascinating invention not least because they are clearly an allegory of humanity: they are sentient beings with language, history and culture, who have their own founding myth that occurred around 33,000 years ago—the time at which humans are commonly believed to have developed. In narrating the *"make-like,"* or metaphor, of their acquisition of *"memory and wakefulness"* to Mary, the mulefas are also used to express a belief in evolution rather than creation—a developmental pattern rather than a god-given one, which is further evidence of Pullman's anti-Church stance (AS, p. 236).

The vision of a disrupted ecosystem is supplemented by other warnings of environmental damage, which form an understated and yet insistent theme in both *The Subtle Knife* and *The Amber Spyglass*. When Asriel harnesses the energy from splitting Roger from his dæmon at the end of *Northern Lights*, in order to open his way to the next world, he unleashes upon his own world the hazards of climate change. Its effects are similar to the implications of real-world global warming, which Will mentions to Lyra, saying that "'people have been interfering with the atmosphere by putting chemicals in it and the weather's going out of control'" (SK, p. 322). In the North of Lyra's world there are thaws and floods, and rivers flowing in the opposite direction to usual. The migration patterns of animals are disturbed. Serafina Pekkala, viewing the damage from her flying vantage point, feels "heartsick," as "The whole of nature was overturned" (AS, p. 39).

On his travels, Will meets a priest with an apocalyptic vision— this environmental change is foretold in the Bible, as "a convulsion in the earth," a turning of rivers:

"All the way from the mountains of central Asia it flowed north for thousands and thousands of years, ever since the Authority of God the Almighty Father created the earth. But when the earth shook and the fog and the floods came, everything changed [. . .] The world is turned upside down." (AS, p. 103)

In his mission to defeat the Authority, Asriel splits the Aurora, with the effect of changing the face of the world that others believe the Authority to have created. Asriel casts himself in the role of a new creator, defiantly "*controlling*" the northern lights (NL, p. 392). This role is questionable, however: Asriel may aspire to creating a republic of heaven but he quite literally risks the earth itself. Asriel's enterprise is therefore a very equivocal one. As Will's father explains to Will and Lyra, Asriel's mission is doomed to failure because a dæmon can only live a full life in the world it was born in—a rule that will have serious implications for Will and Lyra at the end of the trilogy. This ruling, as John Parry explains, dooms Asriel's ambitions, as "'we have to build the republic of heaven where we are, because for us there is no elsewhere'" (AS, p. 382). Pullman's affirmation of the here and now in *His Dark Materials* is one of the strongest messages of the trilogy. Human morality is not invested in another world, or in an afterlife. As Lyra says to Pan in the very final section of *The Amber Spyglass*:

"He meant the kingdom was over, the kingdom of heaven, it was all finished. We shouldn't live as if it mattered more than life in this world, because where we are is always the most important place." (AS, p. 548)

Lyra's emancipation of the dead from the underworld also connects, then, to the environmental morality of *His Dark Materials*, thus (ironically) fulfilling the Bible's myth of Dust that Asriel reads to Lyra. As Lyra explains to the fearful dead:

"When you go out of here, all the particles that make you up will loosen and float apart, just like your dæmons did. [. . .] But your dæmons en't just *nothing* now; they're part of everything. All the atoms that were them, they've gone into the air and the wind and the trees and the earth and all the living things. They'll never vanish. They're just part of everything. And that's exactly what'll happen to you, I swear to you, I promise on my honour. You'll drift apart, it's true, but you'll be out in the open, part of everything alive again." (AS, p. 335)

Lyra's explanation of their future as once more part of the living world is achieved, and people are indeed connected to the "air and the wind and the trees and the earth."

Pullman's Politics

The characters and events of *His Dark Materials* are, then, intensely political in nature. Behind the motivations of the characters, though, is their author's politics. The stories, for example, that Asriel narrates to Ruta Skadi of the burning alive of witches—a part of the history of the real world—demonstrate Pullman's very anti-Church stance. The rewriting of the Fall as a positive and necessary part of the myth of humanity promotes curiosity and knowledge as virtues, with "'the history of human life [as] a struggle between wisdom and stupidity'" (AS, p. 506). At the very end of *The Amber Spyglass*, the morality of the trilogy is made yet more apparent, as Lyra and Pan discuss the building of their own republic of heaven:

"We have to be all those difficult things like cheerful and kind and curious and brave and patient, and we've got to study and think, and work hard, all of us, in all our different worlds" (AS, p. 548)

Through passages such as this, through his emphasis on the virtues of bravery and loyalty, through his depictions of religion and his re-writing of the Fall, through his assault on authority and the Authority, and through his own doctrine of the power of storytelling, Pullman preaches his own politics. This is a political and moral agenda which is emphatically inserted into *His Dark Materials*, a method of storytelling that could well be described as didactic, as the next section explores, alongside further ideas about story.

Story

The Morality of Storytelling

"*Tell them stories*": such is the lesson that Lyra teaches the dead. Her ally Tialys negotiates with the harpies that, in return for listening to the stories of the dead, they will lead them out to rejoin the outside world. Yet, as Lyra herself learns, there is an added dimension to the morality of storytelling. For when she attempts to tell the harpies another of her grand tales of "*parents dead; family treasure; ship-wreck; escape . . .*" (AS, p. 307), the harpy No-Name flies at her in anger, screaming "'Liar!,'" "so that *Lyra* and *liar* were one and the same thing" (AS, p. 308). Lyra must learn to tell the truth, the virtues of narrating simple descriptions of the Oxford landscape where she grew up, "the smells around the place: the smoke from the kilns, the rotten-leaf-mould smell of the river when the wind was in the south-west, the warm smell of the baking potatoes the clay-burners used to eat; and the sound of the water slipping slickly over the sluices" (AS, p. 330). Far from her tales of high adventure, the stories that draw the dead in, that please the harpies, are of a more mundane, but more truthful existence. As No-Name explains, it is this quality that saves Lyra and the dead:

"Because it was true," said No-Name. "Because she spoke the truth. Because it was nourishing. Because it was feeding us. Because we couldn't help it. Because it was true. Because we had no idea that there was anything but wickedness. Because it brought us news of the world and the sun and the wind and the rain. Because it was true." (AS, pp. 332–3)

The emancipation of this truth-telling, not Asriel's high-minded ideals, will defeat the powers of the Church. As Tialys realizes, " 'This will undo everything. It's the greatest blow you could strike. The Authority will be powerless after this.' " (AS, p. 326) Storytelling acquires its own morality. And so it is that Lyra teaches the dead to tell stories, who then teach Mary, who, in turn, tells her story of "Marzipan" to Lyra, through which Lyra realizes her destiny as the new Eve. Storytelling is subsumed into the narrative of *His Dark Materials* as a theme as well as a technique, as in Pullman's *Clockwork*.

Yet the morality of storytelling in *His Dark Materials* could be perceived as being in contradiction to its own narrative line which, like Lyra's favored tales, is brimming with high adventure and fantastical creatures. There is a tension within the trilogy between the excitement of the plotting, the sheer inventiveness of the writing, and a simpler, calmer life. This calmer life is advocated through the harpies' demand to the dead to tell the truth, through the ending of the trilogy, in which Lyra and Will are separated, and Lyra decides she will go to school, and through the peaceful existence of the mulefas.

Although these patterns of existence have psychological realism and emotional truth, their appeal to the reader is perhaps less than that of the world-traversing excitements of other parts of the work. It can be argued that the excitement of the rest of the trilogy has its own form of psychological realism: indeed the argument that Pullman makes against Tolkein is that *The Lord of the Rings* is fantasy with "nothing about people in it," whereas *His Dark Materials* consistently displays a fascination with character. Yet the tension between excitement and acceptance remains. The combination of these two modes of being is another paradox in the trilogy, and yet in the narrative drive toward conclusion, and toward what happens as Lyra and Will grow up and separate, insists on a particular form of morality.

The End

The ending of *His Dark Materials* is worth considering in detail, for what it reveals both about the themes and the storytelling techniques of the trilogy. The end occurs in another garden—the Botanic Garden in Oxford—but unlike the earlier scene in the little wood, Lyra and Will must take the decision to separate from one another forever. Their special powers are lost to them: Will's knife is broken; and Lyra finds she can no longer read the alethiometer. Both must return to their own worlds, and take up their lives again, although older and wiser. In one sense, the separation Lyra and Will must undergo is a terrible denial of their love and sexual feeling for one another, and their acceptance of the simple lives they will now lead is a denial of the high excitement of the plot of *His Dark Materials*.

The choice they make to separate will allow the angels to close up all the windows between worlds, to prevent the seepage of Dust, and the creation of the horrifying Spectres. Choice, as the earlier discussion of "phase space" indicated, is an important moral theme in the trilogy. As the angel Xaphania says to Will, when he pronounces that "'Whatever I do, I will choose it, no one else,'" making informed and moral choices is "'the first step[. . .] toward wisdom'" (AS, p. 525). The ending of the trilogy is so heart-rending precisely because of Lyra and Will's assumption of their own responsibility, and their consequent act of self-denial.

Yet there is a dilemma within the choice that Lyra and Will make. It is their choice to separate, but it is the only choice that they—as the brave, thoughtful beings of Pullman's moral universe—could make. As the angels tell them, only one window can remain open—either the window for the dead to escape or one through which they can be together. The choice is an excruciating one, but they can really only decide to leave the window for the dead.

This paradox of choice is similar to the idea of destiny in the trilogy. Fra Pavel, who reads the Consistorial Court's alethiometer, explains how it works in relation to the future, and Lyra's destiny as the new Eve:

"Please, remember—the alethiometer does not *forecast*; it says, '*If* certain things come about, *then* the consequences will be—' and so on." (AS, p. 71)

The fulfillment of Lyra's destiny is under threat throughout the course of the trilogy, not least from the murderous intentions of the Consistorial Court itself in the shape of Father Gomez, and the bomb directed at her from Saint-Jean-les-Eaux. As the reader of the books travels through the trilogy, Lyra's destiny is indeed uncertain: gradually revealed, and frequently at risk. However, in terms of the "phase space" of the novel, destiny has already been achieved, and the decisions have already been taken—not by Lyra and Will—but by Philip Pullman. Similarly, Lyra and Will's characters determine that the only choice they can make at the end is the right choice—to stay apart.

Unlike the enfeebled Authority, then, Pullman—as the creator of the trilogy—despite illustrating multiple options for his characters, actually inscribes their choice as an inevitability. For them to be proper heroes of *His Dark Materials*, and the rightful creators of their own republics of heaven, their characters will dictate their actions. Pullman discussed this inevitability of the storyteller's creation in his lecture "Let's Write It in Red." The implication of phase space is that "a path is a path *to*: it has a destination":

For every story has to have an ending. Sometimes you know what the ending is before you begin. Well and good. Sometimes you don't, and then you have to wander about through the events until you manage to see the natural destination. But once you know where it is, you must make for it, and then go back and clear the path and make sure that every twist and turn is there because you want it to be [. . .] In other words you must design the path so that it leads to the destination most surely, and with the maximum effect.

Ultimately, the role of the creator is in conflict with characters' free will, as Milton's Adam and Eve discover. Lyra and Will, although not controlled by the Authority, are nonetheless controlled by an authority external to the text—that of the author himself. It is the author, then, who controls the narrative. Narrative choices develop from his own sense of morality, and hence didacticism is an integral feature of the trilogy.

Pullman as Storyteller

Pullman—as the reviews discussed in the next chapter attest—is a consummate storyteller. In several interviews, he has exemplified the effect of storytelling through the story of his nightly version of Homer's *Odyssey* on his young son: "'By the end of the story, Tom, who was sitting with a glass in his hand, was so galvanized he bit a chunk out of the glass.'" (Robert McCrum, "Dæmon Geezer," *Observer*). Pullman's analysis of the power of storytelling is, with regard to his own talents, acute. *His Dark Materials* is constructed on a series of cliff-hangers, shifts in narrative perspective, and characters with whose fates readers are deeply concerned. The wealth of intertextual reference in the trilogy also establishes Pullman's mastery over narrative through his incorporation of many other texts and stories within his own. The scenes in the land of the dead in *The Amber Spyglass* are one extremely rich example, populated as they are by characters developed from Greek mythology: the boatman who takes them across the river is akin to Charon, who rows across the river Styx to the underworld, while the harpies are Homeric. As well as the echoes of Milton, Blake and von Kleist, there are nods to science fiction, to the traditions of children's literature and—in the attempt to stop the bomb seconds before its explosion in Saint-Jean-les-Eaux—to the James Bond-style thriller. Through his storytelling, Pullman enthrals and incorporates, reworking and remaking narrative.

Storytelling has another purpose in *His Dark Materials*, however, and that purpose is didactic. In reading the trilogy, an impassioned sense of the author's morality develops: the anti-Church stance, the importance of individual responsibility, and the paths that Lyra and Will must follow, as Xaphania explains to them:

"Dust is not a constant. There's not a fixed quantity that has always been the same. Conscious beings make Dust—they renew it all the time, by thinking and feeling and reflecting, by gaining wisdom and passing it on.

"And if you help everyone else in your worlds to do that, by helping them to learn and understand about themselves and each other and the way everything works, and by showing them how to be kind instead of cruel, and patient instead of hasty, and cheerful instead of surly, and above all how to keep their minds open and free and curious . . . Then they will renew enough to replace what is lost through one window." (AS, p. 520)

Dust, then, is created by human goodness, though this is goodness of a liberal and thoughtful kind rather than a goodness sanctioned by the sexually repressive Church. The tone here seems almost to be that of a kindly headmaster, indicating Pullman's didactic purpose quite clearly. The message, though, is hidden within the stories, rather than hammered from the pulpit. In the acceptance speech he made for the Carnegie Medal in 1996, Pullman discussed the potential for story to deliver effective lessons in morality:

> All stories teach, whether the storyteller intends them to or not. They teach the world we create. They teach the morality we live by. They teach it much more effectively than moral precepts and instructions. [. . .]
>
> We don't need lists of rights and wrongs, tables of do's and don'ts: we need books, time, and silence. Thou shalt not is soon forgotten, but Once upon a time lasts forever.

Pullman is thus an evangelist for story, and in his stories provides his own vision of morality. But what is the role of the reader within this moral universe? How might the reader react to the didacticism of any story, and of *His Dark Materials* in particular?

Loose Ends

The debates that rage around *His Dark Materials*—which are addressed more fully in the next chapter—suggest that there are a variety of different ways in which the role of the reader is configured in *His Dark Materials*. The variety of these configurations has been influenced by different readers' reactions to the didacticism of the trilogy, and particularly to the portrayals of religion and to the politics of the republic of heaven.

There is a further way in which readers can find their place within *His Dark Materials*. This is through loose ends, and through the gaps and silences that—if it is thoroughly searched—can be discovered in the trilogy. One such is the veil of modesty that Pullman draws over Lyra and Will's temptation and fall in the wood. What, actually, do they do? This is implied, rather than told. The nearest the narrative actually gets to describing full-on sex, comes later:

Knowing exactly what he was doing and exactly what it would mean, he moved his hand from Lyra's wrist and stroked the red-gold fur of her dæmon.

Lyra gasped. But her surprise was mixed with a pleasure so like the joy that flooded through her when she had put the fruit to his lips that she couldn't protest, because she was breathless. With a racing heart she responded in the same way: she put her hand on the silky warmth of Will's dæmon, and as her fingers tightened in the fur she knew that Will was feeling exactly what she was.

And she knew too that neither dæmon would change now, having felt a lover's hands on them. These were their shapes for life: they would want no other. (AS, pp. 527–8)

As a metaphor of sexual union, this moment is also entirely in keeping with the laws Pullman sets up regarding dæmons. The two are named as lovers, and their dæmons' settling marks their ultimate transition to adulthood. The structure of metaphor means that a sexual act is not directly described, however, and so readers must make their own interpretation. This could be thought of as prudishness—the trilogy, after all, is ostensibly written for children and it could be thought that modesty prevents the description of the act. Pullman's espousal of adolescent sexuality would seem to make this unlikely, however. Instead, rather than slavishly following the politics of the celebration of human sexuality through explicit description, metaphor—and the *poetics* of the trilogy—intervenes. This is an instance of Pullman leaving the narrative open to interpretation, in comparison to some of the more explicitly didactic sections.

Another example of the gaps left for readers' interpretation is in the depiction of Lord Asriel and his battle for the republic of heaven.

In terms of narrative technique, the depiction of Asriel is a fascinating one, as throughout *The Subtle Knife*, although central to the plot, he only ever appears at second hand, through the reports of his servant, and of Ruta Skadi. When his preparations for war take center stage in *The Amber Spyglass*, Asriel appears again in person. Yet the way in which the political struggle for the universe is portrayed—with Asriel, but also with Mrs. Coulter, and the Magisterium—is to shift their activities in and out of focus, to foreground or to hide them. It is through the use of an omniscient narrator that Pullman enables himself to do this. However, this is an omniscient narrator who does not narrate everything, and leaves open questions. After the defeat of both the Authority and his regent Metatron, but also the deaths of Lord Asriel and Mrs. Coulter, to whom will governance of the worlds fall? Lyra and Will will attempt to build their own republics of heaven, but these are very different entities to the political structure envisioned by Asriel. What will happen to the remaining forces of war, both on the side of Asriel and on that of the Magisterium? The dead are emancipated, and so fear is banished from the worlds, but these questions are not resolved any more than the futures of Lyra and Will, as young adults in their separate worlds, are.

These uncertainties, these loose ends, are compelling places for the reader of *His Dark Materials* to consider for two reasons. The first is to do with the potential further interventions by Philip Pullman in his own creation—in numerous reports he has suggested possible developments (though not necessarily sequels) of the stories and characters of *His Dark Materials*. The second is more to do with readers' capacity for imaginative engagement with the themes and concerns of the novels. Pullman makes the plea in his Carnegie speech for "books, time, and silence." Through the loose ends of his trilogy, for the spaces in which readers are asked to think for themselves and to let fly their own imaginative capacities, Pullman proves in *His Dark Materials* his own adage of "Once upon a time lasts for ever."

3

The Novels' Reception

In an attempt, perhaps, to match Philip Pullman's own capacious vocabulary, critics have reached for the thesaurus in their reviews of *His Dark Materials*. Terence Blacker in the UK's *Mail on Sunday* spoke of *Northern Lights* as "mesmerising, spectacular," and went on to describe *The Subtle Knife* as "a genuine masterpiece of intelligent, imaginative storytelling, a multi-layered quest and adventure story." Peter Kemp in the UK's *Sunday Times* wrote of *The Subtle Knife* that "Marvels and monsters, tragedies and triumphs are unrolled with a lavishness typical of this prodigiously gifted author." For Claire Dederer, writing in the US *Newsday*, *Northern Lights* is "a ripping yarn with diabolical cleverness and angelic clarity," and *The Amber Spyglass* "brilliantly completes the preceding books and casts a reflected glory upon them." Michael Dirda, one of Pullman's biggest advocates in the US, wrote in the *Washington Post* of *The Amber Spyglass* that "Pullman's sheer storytelling power [is] sinfully irresistible [. . . it is] a novel of electrifying power and splendor, deserving celebration, as violent as a fairy tale and as shocking as art must be."

From some of the earliest reviews of the *Northern Lights*, the critics also began to mark out the trilogy—even before the second and third volumes had been published—for classic status alongside some of the established greats of children's literature. Dirda wrote in his review of *Northern Lights* in 1996 that if its sequel were to be "as good as *The Golden Compass*, we'll be two thirds of the way to the completion of a modern fantasy classic." He felt his own predictions to be justified by the appearance of *The Subtle Knife*, affirming both that *Northern Lights* "can be mentioned in the same breath as such classics as Madeleine L'Engle's *A Wrinkle in Time*, Philippa Pearce's *Tom's Midnight Garden*, and Alan Garner's *The Owl Service*. . . . Actually, Pullman's book is more breathtakingly, all-stops-out thrilling than any of them," and that its sequel is "just as quick-moving and unputdownable as its predecessor." Gregory Maguire, reviewing *The Subtle Knife* in the *New York Times*, recommended that the reader "Put Philip Pullman on the shelf with Ursula K. Le Guin, Susan Cooper, Lloyd Alexander, at least until we get to see Volume 3." Sarah Johnson, in *The Times* (UK), believed that the trilogy "promises to live alongside the works of Tolkein and C. S. Lewis as an icon of imaginative writing for children. It's a claim made for many books but it is to be taken seriously in Philip Pullman's case, because of the depth of his vision."

By the publication of *The Amber Spyglass*, the pattern was set for the nomination of the trilogy for a place in posterity. Matt Berman, writing in the New Orleans *Times-Picayune*, said that *The Amber Spyglass* "completes the finest and most original fantasy series since *The Lord of the Rings*." Boyd Tonkin in the UK's *Independent* also referred to Tolkein and Lewis in his assessment of *His Dark Materials*, declaring that, "These three books deserve a place alongside [. . .] *The Lord of the Rings* and [. . .] *The Chronicles of Narnia* as classic attempts to restore debate about the meaning of life to a culture that often drowns in trivia." Andrew Marr in the UK *Daily Telegraph* judged the trilogy to be "one of the greatest adventure stories I've ever read," leading to his assertion that it "will be being bought,

and pulled, dog-eared from family bookshelves, in 100 years' time."
Opinions about the trilogy's potential for being read years into the
future is summed up by Carla Mckay in the UK's *Daily Mail*: "it
tells an incredible story—one that will harness the imaginations of
children and adults now and in future generations."

Tolkein and Lewis were not the only authors mentioned as reference points for *His Dark Materials*, as many critics would refer to
the trilogy's intertextuality. Milton and Blake were obvious points
of reference, but some cast the net wider. Andrew Marr mentioned
Milton, Dickens, Michael Moorcock and, in the depiction of the
land of the dead, traces of prison camps, Dante and Dore. Michael
Dirda reeled off a whole list of intertextual references:

Besides finding hints of *Paradise Lost* and Blake's poetry, the astute will pick
up echoes of the following: Christ's harrowing of Hell, Jewish Kabbala (the
legend of the god-like angel Metatron), Gnostic doctrine (Dust, our sleeping
souls needing to be awakened), the "death of God" controversy, *Perelandra*,
the Oz books (the Wheelers), Wagners' *Ring of the Nibelungs* (Siegfried's
mending of the sword), Aeneas, Odysseus and Dante in the Underworld, the
Grail legend and the wounded Fisher King, Peter Pan, Wordsworth's panthe-
istic "Immortality Ode," the doctrine of the hidden God and speculation
about the plurality of worlds, situational ethics (actions, not people, being
good or bad), the cessation of miracles, "Star Wars," colonialist evangelizing,
the fetch of British folklore, the 17th-century doctrine of sympathies (for the
Gallivespian communication device, the lodestone-resonator), the popular
mythology of the Jesuits as ascetic masterminds of realpolitik, superhero comics and even Pullman's own early novel for adults, *Galatea*. Fans of science
fiction and fantasy may also detect undertones of Ursula Le Guin's Earthsea
books, Fritz Leiber's sword-and-sorcery tales of Fafhrd and the Gray Mouser,
Jack Vance's elegant Dying Earth stories.

This esoteric and eclectic list is only a start to the intertextual source
spotting, but it demonstrates both critics' appreciation of and engagement with the trilogy. The overwhelmingly positive reaction

with which the trilogy was greeted is based upon several factors. The predominant one, as demonstrated by the reviews already quoted here, is to do with Pullman's storytelling prowess. Further plaudits come from Susanna Rustin in the UK *Financial Times*, who defined Pullman as "a charismatic storyteller," from Margo Jefferson in the *New York Times*, who described *His Dark Materials* as "a narrative of tremendous pace," and from Stephanie Loer of the *Boston Globe*, for whom the trilogy was "a roller-coaster of an adventure story." However, some dissenting voices would be heard about the plotting of *The Amber Spyglass*. Claudia Fitzherbert in the *Daily Telegraph* called it "a great baggy mess of a book. Threads left lying about in the two previous volumes of the trilogy are picked up and re-examined but there's not a lot of tying up." S. F. Said, writing in the same newspaper, thought *The Amber Spyglass* "perhaps the weakest of the three parts," despite saying it "richly deserves to win the Whitbread." Indeed, general opinion about the trilogy is that *The Amber Spyglass*, despite becoming the winner of the Whitbread Book of the Year Award, does not function well as a stand-alone book, and is the least successfully plotted. Only occasionally did critics perceive a potential irony in Pullman's virtuoso storytelling and the message of the trilogy. Nicolette Jones, writing a very perceptive critique in the *Sunday Times*, commented that "The book's message is that we have only one life and it is on earth [. . .] But this sits awkwardly with a creation that has made us believe in several parallel universes, and which can imagine so comprehensively the land of the dead. The theme of the book suddenly seems at odds with its method." Nonetheless, this paradox did not lessen Jones's largely positive review.

The second main factor for the highly appreciative response to the trilogy is to do with its engagement with "big ideas." This, though, would also be the cause of dissent, due to the highly contentious nature of many of these big ideas. As Nick Thorpe put it in the *Sunday Times*, "while his primary passion is storytelling, his battle is nothing if not ideological." S. F. Said spoke of the trilogy "prob[ing] some of the most fundamental questions of human existence." Andrew Marr saw Pullman as concerned with the big ideas of "love, moral conduct, power, nature, paradise, hell and the existence or otherwise of God, the universe and everything." As Michael Dirda ends his review of *Northern Lights* by suggesting, the first book asks a series of questions, that "offer moral complexity [. . .] What do you do when people you love turn out to be evil? Do admirable goals ever justify despicable means? What is the proper place of religion and science in civil life? How does one deal with betrayal?"

The question of the "proper place of religion" would become one of the most controversial elements of the trilogy, and is considered later in this chapter. The critics' analysis of the trilogy's engagement with moral and metaphysical questions is crucial in determining the factors contributing to its remarkable success. For many, the intellectually-engaged nature of Pullman's work marked a distinction between it and much writing directed at adults. As Terence Blacker phrased it in his review of *The Subtle Knife*, "At a time when English fiction is widely perceived as being parochial in its concerns and domestic in its settings, one Englishman is at work on a towering trilogy of novels." Moreover, in *The Times*, Erica Wagner proclaimed that *His Dark Materials* "looks set to pull down the whole moral framework that has underpinned Western civilization. Who says English writers aren't ambitious anymore?" This commentary echoed the provocative remarks made by Pullman himself on acceptance of the Carnegie Medal for *Northern Lights* (and quoted in Chapter 1), and in "Let's Write it in Red," where he said that "Children's books, [. . .] at this time in our literary history, open out on wideness and amplitude—a moral and mental spaciousness—that adult fiction seems to have turned its back on."

The reversal of expectation inherent in Pullman's comments, and those of Wagner and Blacker, signal another vital aspect of the reception of the trilogy. *His Dark Materials* is classified as a work of children's literature, with its primary market among teenagers and young adults. Pullman, despite his early authorship of two novels for adults, is known as a writer for children, and has become a champion of children's literature. However, children's literature—along with genre literature—has regularly been granted less attention than literary fiction. The coverage given to various types of fiction in the pages of any newspaper demonstrates this very clearly—books for children, or science fiction, or romance, consistently receive much less space than more "serious" works. Pullman has addressed this prejudice in two ways: firstly through his comments in numerous speeches, interviews and opinion pieces, in which he elevates children's literature above the mass of literary fiction; and secondly, through *His Dark Materials* itself, and the way in which it has been critically received. Nicolette Jones, writing in the *Sunday Times*, stated that *His Dark Materials* "earned him a place in the firmament of children's literature," but also that it "blurred distinctions between writing for children and writing for adults, and between genre fantasy and fiction of general appeal." In an article specifically addressing the issue of the divide between children's and adults' writing, the UK *Observer*'s Robert McCrum stressed the need for Pullman to be "evaluated as an important contemporary novelist who happens to write in a certain genre, a significant writer to be spoken of in the same breath as, say, Beryl Bainbridge, A. S. Byatt or Salman Rushdie."

Some of the response to Pullman's writing has been set against the context of a rising interest in children's literature in the 1990s and 2000s, and in comparison to another phenomenal children's writer: J. K. Rowling, the author of the *Harry Potter* novels (1997–   ). Rowling and Pullman are at the forefront of rising interest in children's books among adult readers, as Boyd Tonkin's *Independent* article "Once Upon a Time in the Marketing Department . . ." exemplified. The sales figures of Pullman's series would undoubtedly suggest that it has an appeal transcending genre and market prejudices.

Several critics have seized on the *Harry Potter* comparison. Robert McCrum saw Pullman as "far superior to Rowling." Michael Dirda noted that "By comparison, the agreeable and entertaining Harry Potter books look utterly innocuous." Nick Thorpe, discussing the metaphysical concerns of the trilogy, stated that "It's ambitious, theologically nuanced stuff which makes Harry Potter look like Noddy." Claudia Fitzherbert wrote in a similar vein when she commented upon the vogue for adults reading children's books that "Adults read J. K. Rowling because she is not complicated; children read Philip Pullman because he is." These comments perhaps do disservice to J. K. Rowling, but the message they convey about *His Dark Materials* is clear: its definition is as a complex, provocative and deeply intellectual work of literature, whether read by children or adults.

The comparison to, and contrast with, C. S. Lewis's *Chronicles of Narnia* has been referred to by numerous critics, and to some has proved a particular cause of provocation, closely linked to Pullman's treatment of religion. It is the establishment of an anti-religious myth in *His Dark Materials* that lead Andrew Marr to comment that "Pullman does for atheism what C. S. Lewis did for God." Peter Hitchens, the *Mail on Sunday* journalist who declared Pullman "the most dangerous author in Britain," specifically couched his condemnation in terms of the C. S. Lewis debate: "one stubborn and important pocket of Christianity survives, in the Narnia stories of C S Lewis. Now here comes an opportunity to dethrone him and supplant his books with others which proclaim the death of God to the young." As Hitchens wrote of *His Dark Materials* in a later *Mail on Sunday* article, "I think these books should carry a strong warning, pointing out that they are deliberate anti-Christian propaganda." Other journalists have protested against Pullman's anti-Church stance. Claudia Fitzherbert, for example, warns, "Christian parents beware: his books can damage your child's faith." Sarah Johnson, who has been a vocal anti-Pullman reviewer despite appreciating his storytelling abilities, wrote in *The Times* that the series is "the most savage attack on organised religion I have ever seen."

The anti-Church ideology of *His Dark Materials* is reflected by numerous epithets given to Pullman by reviewers. The *Guardian* named him "a heretical fantasist"; Jessica Mann in the *Sunday Telegraph* called him a "militant atheist"; and Nick Thorpe dubbed him an "anti-Christian fundamentalist." Michael Dirda comments that "In another time, this [*The Amber Spyglass*] is a book that would have made the Index [the Catholic list of prohibited texts], and in still another era gotten its author condemned to the stake as a heretic." Ideological passions have been roused by the series, with reviewers making it very clear the extent of Pullman's attack on the Church and organized religion.

There has been a question over Pullman's even-handedness in his portrayals of Church figures, which has been asked by both advocates of and detractors from the series. Critics have made the comment that the clerics of the Magisterium are the only characters in the trilogy who are not allowed a fully-rounded existence. Nick Thorpe, in his very thoughtful *Sunday Times* article, commented on "the almost pantomime evil of his churchmen, who are conspicuously lacking in either redeeming features or consequently the nuanced psychology that make his heroes so compelling." In the *Daily Telegraph*, Melanie McDonagh disliked the series for its portrayal of the Catholic Church. She saw Pullman's representations in a tradition of "Protestant-atheist polemic" in which "the Catholic Church is seen as a diabolic institution, all Spanish Inquisition and sex-obsessed celibates." Claudia Fitzherbert commented that "nearly all of his villains have moments of pathos and/or greatness, except for the priests." Erica Wagner wrote that "the Church he portrays becomes so over-the-top wicked it threatens to tip into caricature."

Such stereotyping fits Pullman's purpose, however. As a consequence, some reviewers have considered the extent of Pullman's didacticism, both in his dismissal of the Church but also in the promotion of his own brand of morality. Angelique Chrisafis termed him "an evangelical atheist" in the *Guardian*, while Jessica Mann claimed that "The moralizing is overt." Erica Wagner linked this specifically to Pullman's previous profession as a teacher, noting that "it is clear he has not quite lost his taste for pedagogy." Brian Alderson in the *New York Times* accused Pullman of "designer theology," and detected a paradox in his position as authorial creator that is unsettling for the reader: "The author as God must lean from his heaven and direct affairs in the way he requires them to go, and we mortal readers must erect small gantries from which to suspend our varieties of disbelief." At least some critics showed uneasiness about Pullman's controlling authorial position.

Some critics linked this to their sense of Pullman's ambition. A writer who sets out to rewrite the Bible and *Paradise Lost*, and peppers his work with epigraphs from famous writers is, as Nicolette Jones phrased it, suffering from "overweening ambition." In places, this ambition was thought to have gone awry—the perceived shapelessness of *The Amber Spyglass*, with its many loose ends, is one example. Erica Wagner also tackled the question of ambition, but was more positive in her conclusions: "A touch of hubris, perhaps, to implicitly compare himself to these authors? Pullman's ambition shines out from him [. . .] This is remarkable writing." Jessica Mann thought Pullman was probably writing with one eye to the future, and to inclusion on school and college reading lists: "I suspect that Pullman, formerly a teacher, expected his book to become a 'set text,' with allusions and parallels clearly signalled." Other reviewers also noted *His Dark Materials*' readiness for interpretation, with Peter Kemp commenting that "Suspense, surprise and eerie poetry coalesce into a terrific tale flickering with allegorical significance (it's no accident that Lyra's most valuable possession is a device for deciphering symbols)." Terence Blacker compounded this sense of the possibilities for studying *His Dark Materials*, saying that "Doubtless, even now, nerdish academics will be earnestly deconstructing the symbols and subtext." Although Blacker's comments might say more about journalists' prejudices about academia than about *His Dark Materials* itself, he is right in suggesting the text's potential place within the academy: dissertations, articles and now books are beginning to be fashioned around Pullman's original creation.

To return to the specific accusation of didacticism, though, sees other critics, such as Christina Hardyment, who described Pullman as "a largely invisible moralist," in more forgiving mood. Others strongly applaud Pullman's moral purpose. Andrew Marr wrote that "What he gives me and what excites me is the sense that a post-Christian world can be as intensely filled with pity, the search for goodness, and an acute awareness of evil, as any religious universe." Indeed, the capacity for Pullman in *His Dark Materials* to address moral issues is affirmed by the critics. In the *Independent*, Natasha Walter set her reaction to *His Dark Materials* against the terrorist attacks in America in 2001, writing that "Isn't this a great vision for the world after 11 September? Here we have a book that asks us to believe that we can build a new, highly moral world without the precepts of religion."

This is indeed a bold claim made for Pullman, but one that he has wanted to take up. In a speech at the Edinburgh Festival of Literature in 2002 on the morality of writing in the context of terrorist threat and looming war with Iraq, Pullman stated that writers must address, as Angelique Crisafis reported, "larger questions of moral conduct" if they were not to "become useless and irrelevant." Whatever else the critics might have said, or still have to say, about Philip Pullman, it is apparent that with *His Dark Materials* he follows his own exhortation. As Erica Wagner put it, "He is a remarkable writer, courageous and dangerous: he reminds us that this is what an artist should be, after all."

4

The Novels' Performance

Since their publication, *Northern Lights*, *The Subtle Knife* and *The Amber Spyglass* have become extremely successful books, both in terms of the number of sales made of the trilogy and with regard to the trilogy's critical success. All three of the books have had long established presences on the *New York Times* and *Sunday Times* Bestseller Lists. The trilogy has been translated into over thirty-five languages, and published in many different countries worldwide.

Philip Pullman has made frequent appearances in the media and on the literary festival circuit, as well as delivering lectures and being invited onto the BBC Radio 4 institution *Desert Island Discs* in 2002. Television programs have also been made to celebrate the achievement of the author of *His Dark Materials*, including a BBC film "The World of Philip Pullman" in 2002 and a *South Bank Show* featuring Pullman in 2003.

Before the completion of the trilogy, Pullman had already been feted by the children's book community for his previous work. *The Firework Maker's Daughter* was a Gold Medal winner at the Smarties Book Prizes. The later *Clockwork* won a Silver Medal at the same awards, and was shortlisted for both the Carnegie Medal and the

Whitbread Children's Book Award. *His Dark Materials* would bring further awards: *Northern Lights* won The Carnegie Medal and the *Guardian* Children's Fiction Award. When, for the first time in 2000, a longlist of that year's Booker Prize was officially published, *The Amber Spyglass* was on the list, though it did not proceed any further to the shortlist. This preliminary incursion onto adult prize lists would soon be repeated in more spectacular fashion with the Whitbread Awards. These prizes are composed of several category awards (for best novel, poetry collection, auto/biography and so on), the winners of which then go forward to be judged for the Whitbread Book of the Year. *The Amber Spyglass* was judged to be the 2001 Whitbread Children's Book of the Year by its category panel. It then went onto to win the overall prize to become Whitbread Book of the Year, an unprecedented act in the face of competition from work written for adults. The award of the Whitbread Book of the Year to Pullman cemented his reputation as a writer with an appeal to children and to adults, but also achieved what Pullman has long claimed that writing for children is capable of—appealing to a multigenerational audience through the virtuosity of its storytelling and the urgency of its themes. For any doubters, the Whitbread Award was a sign that Pullman—and children's literature more generally—should be taken seriously. When Pullman was granted the Eleanor Farjeon Award at the end of 2002, it was very suitably in recognition for his achievement in altering adult perceptions of children's books.

There are various plans to adapt *His Dark Materials* for different media. A BBC Radio dramatization has already been aired in January 2003. Each part of the trilogy was adapted by Lavinia Murray into a two-and-a-half hour episode, with a cast starring Lulu Popplewell as Lyra, Daniel Anthony as Will, Terence Stamp as Lord Asriel and Emma Fielding as Mrs. Coulter. In the adaptation, a narrator's role was given to the angel Balthamos, and Mrs. Coulter's dæmon, who remains nameless in the novels, was given the name Ozymandias.

The National Theatre in London plans a stage version of *His Dark Materials* in Autumn 2003. Nicholas Hytner, the Director, has been quoted in the *Daily Telegraph* as saying that the adaptation will be "big, adventurous and conceptually extravagant. The books are unstageable, so that should keep me busy." The novels are to be adapted into two plays by Nicholas Wright.

Films of the trilogy are also planned. New Line, the production company who made the very successful *Lord of the Rings* adaptations in the 2000s have bought the rights, and production is due to begin in the period 2003/4. The company's imaginative use of CGI (computer generated imagery) will undoubtedly play a large role in the creation of a convincing screen presence for the dæmons and alternate worlds of *His Dark Materials*. The playwright Tom Stoppard is writing the screenplay, and various high-profile directors have been mentioned in association with the project.

In October 2003, another *His Dark Materials* volume will appear. *Lyra's Oxford* is set after the end of *The Amber Spyglass*, and promises to be a celebration of her home city. It will include a short story which begins with Lyra once more on the roofs of Oxford with her dæmon. The story is illustrated with wood-blocks by the artist John Lawrence, and also includes pull-out maps of Lyra's Oxford.

Another book with a *His Dark Materials* connection is due to be published by the end of 2003. *The Science of His Dark Materials* by the science writers John and Mary Gribbin will include an introduction by Pullman and will explore the scientific basis of the trilogy, including parallel universes and the northern lights.

In numerous interviews, Pullman has also mentioned plans for writing a full-length book based in the worlds of the trilogy. *The Book of Dust*, the proposed title for the next volume, will not be a sequel, but may well contain earlier adventures of Lee Scoresby and Iorek Byrnison, and the love story of Serafina Pekkala. Pullman has also suggested that the adventures of Pantalaimon and Will's dæmon

Kirjava, after they are separated from Lyra and Will on the riverbank, might be part of the continuing tales of *His Dark Materials*. Any further stories from Pullman's pen, particularly if based in Lyra and Will's worlds, are awaited with great expectation. Indeed, some have not been content with waiting, and role-playing game websites have been set up, so fans themselves can play out the future of the republic of heaven (see the bibliography for details). Any future writing from Pullman himself will be eagerly received, carefully read and comprehensively judged. And yet it would seem certain that with the majestic, provocative and thrilling *His Dark Materials*, Philip Pullman has already written a place for his heroes, and himself, in the literary history books.

5

Further Reading and Discussion Questions

In this section, you will find a series of questions and discussion topics on the *His Dark Materials* trilogy. Some of these relate to points that have been raised in previous chapters, while others give some ideas for your own exploration. There are also some suggestions for further reading, including other creative works that make interesting comparisons to *Northern Lights*, *The Subtle Knife* and *The Amber Spyglass*, and works of non-fiction that illuminate the novels' contexts. The section ends with a bibliography of Pullman's work and selected criticism and interviews.

Storytelling

1. *"Tell them stories"* is an insistent refrain throughout the trilogy. What are the various kinds of storytelling that are encountered in the course of the narrative?

2. Lyra is a consummate storyteller—Iorek Byrnison even renames her "Lyra Silvertongue." Yet her stories are frequently lies, and in a section of *The Amber Spyglass* "Lyra" and *"liar"* become

"one and the same thing." Is she right to lie? Under what situations is her lying justified? When should she tell the truth, and why? What are the responsibilities of storytelling? Think about the scene in the world of the dead, when Lyra tells stories to the dead and the harpies. What is the difference between these two modes of storytelling? Why does one succeed where the other fails?

3. Pullman writes beautifully of the joys of storytelling: "As she said that, as she took charge, part of her felt a little stream of pleasure rising upwards in her breast like the bubbles of champagne." How do you think this, and other reactions to storytelling encountered in the trilogy, might relate to Pullman's own beliefs about his work? For further ideas, read Pullman's shorter novel *Clockwork*, a book which is a metaphor about storytelling.

4. What are the techniques Pullman uses to tell the story of *His Dark Materials*? As one story broken into three different parts, how does he sustain the narrative? How does he introduce new characters? How successfully is the story carried over the course of three volumes? Does he tie up all the loose ends in the third volume?

Dæmons

5. The first words of the *His Dark Materials* trilogy are "Lyra and her dæmon." What is a "dæmon"? How does a dæmon reveal the character of its human? In numerous interviews, Pullman has described the dæmon as the best idea he's ever had. Why are the dæmons such a great device in the trilogy? How do they function both in terms of characterization and in the plot?

6. Certain characters in the trilogy do not have dæmons, or have a different relationship to them. Humans from Will's world do not have them. Armored bears don't either, though Iofur Raknison wants one. The witches can separate from their dæmons in a

way that humans cannot. What other examples can you think of? How do these variable relationships demonstrate the flexibility of Pullman's idea?

7. When Lyra discusses with the Able-Seaman the "settling" of dæmons during adolescence, he says that "'There's plenty of folk as'd like to have a lion as a dæmon and they end up with a poodle. And till they learn to be satisfied with what they are, they're going to be fretful about it. Waste of feeling, that is.'" (*NL*, p. 167) What do different characters' dæmons in the trilogy tell the reader about them? Why are "almost all servants' dæmons" dogs? (*NL*, p. 5) What space does this sort of determinism allow for characters to change? How do their dæmons come to settle in their permanent form?

8. From what the Able-Seaman says, a human does not choose the final form of his or her own dæmon. Yet if the dæmon's settling is due to both a person's character and past actions, how would your own dæmon be determined? Others that you know? When pressed in interview, Pullman has suggested that his would be "a magpie or a jackdaw, one of those birds that pick up bright shining things" (in Helena de Bertadano, *Sunday Telegraph*). From what you know about him, do you think he's got it right?

Gender

9. The trilogy has two protagonists—the female Lyra and the male Will. How are their respective roles as heroine and hero portrayed, and how does this reflect upon the representation of the sexes in the novels generally? Do you think Lyra and Will's characters are gender-stereotyped at all? If so, how? If not, why not? At the very beginning of *Northern Lights*, Lord Asriel hurts Lyra by twisting her arm: "It might have been enough to make

her cry, if she were the sort of girl who cried." (*NL*, p. 15) In what ways does Pullman construct and deconstruct notions of gender identity? When Lyra meets Will, she begins to lose some of her independence as a female. For example, at the beginning of *The Amber Spyglass* she has to be rescued by him from the fairy-tale-like sleep under which Mrs. Coulter is holding her captive. Do you agree with this interpretation?

10. The dæmons of Lyra's world are the opposite sex to their human. Why is this? What does this say about human character, and Pullman's concept of the dæmon?

11. Mrs. Coulter is one of the most striking characters in *His Dark Materials*. She is glamorous, cunning and evil—an archetype of a certain sort of femininity. What do you think about this portrayal? What about when she eventually—and very unexpectedly—begins to have maternal feelings for Lyra in *The Amber Spyglass*? Is she to be trusted? How does she compare as a character to the woman who brought Lyra up, Ma Costa?

12. "'Eve! Mother of all! Eve, again! Mother Eve!'" This is Lyra's destiny. But what is the difference between the Eve of the Bible and of *Paradise Lost*, and Lyra as a new Eve? In changing the role of Eve, how is Pullman altering negative perceptions of women? Could this be termed a "feminist" rewriting of Eve's role? Compare Pullman's reinscription of Eve with that of feminist writer Angela Carter in *The Passion of New Eve* (1977).

Innocence and Experience

13. Lyra is described by Farder Coram as a "'strange innocent creature.'" What sort of innocence is this? How is innocence contrasted with experience in the trilogy? How does this relate to Lyra's destiny in the final volume of the trilogy, and her great betrayal? What is this betrayal, and why is it necessary?

14. Will and Lyra are attacked by "a single mass" of children in Cittàgazze, "snatching, threatening, screaming, spitting" (*SK*, p. 241). Will has seen children acting this way before, in his own world. Is innocence, and the state of childhood, then, necessarily good? How do the terms "good" and "evil" relate to the terms "innocence" and "experience," "childhood" and "adulthood"? The gang mentality of the children is similar to that portrayed by William Golding in *The Lord of the Flies* (1954), and debated by Blake Morrison in his meditation on the real-life case of the two child killers of an even younger child in *As If* (1997), a book Pullman has said he admires greatly.

15. Lyra, like another famous hero of children's literature, Peter Pan (in J. M. Barrie's *Peter Pan in Kensington Gardens* (1906)), doesn't want things to change or to grow up: she "wished passionately that nothing had changed, nothing would ever change, that she could be Lyra of Jordan College for ever and ever." (*NL*, p. 151) Yet as the trilogy proceeds, it charts a voyage for both Lyra and Will from innocence to experience, and from childhood to adulthood. Why does Lyra initially resist the process of growing up, and how does she come to accept it? What are the advantages of adulthood, and of a human's dæmon becoming fixed? How does this relate to the development of human character and morality?

16. The Magisterium decides that Dust is "'the physical evidence for original sin'" (*NL*, p. 371), brought into the world by the first Adam and Eve eating the forbidden fruit. Mrs. Coulter justifies her work severing children from their dæmons for the General Oblation Board by preventing the passage from innocence to experience. She explains to Lyra, "'You see, your dæmon's a wonderful friend and companion when you're young, but at the age we call puberty, the age you're coming to very soon, darling, dæmons bring all sort of troublesome

thoughts and feelings, and that's what lets Dust in.'" How, then, is the onset of sexual maturity integrated into the plot and themes of *His Dark Materials*? In your opinion, does Pullman resist or celebrate these "'troublesome thoughts and feelings'"? Does this contrast with the treatment of other children's writers on the theme of growing up? Think particularly about the story Mary tells of how she stopped being a nun in the chapter "Marzipan." What effect does this "new knowledge" have on Lyra? (*AS*, p. 471)

Religion and the Church

17. The *Catholic Herald* declared that *His Dark Materials* should be "thrown on the bonfire," and Peter Hitchens, writing in the *Mail on Sunday*, termed Pullman "the most dangerous author in Britain." The trilogy has incited this hostile opposition through its extremely negative portrayal of religion and the Church. What do you think of Pullman's representations? Why are they so controversial? What is it that Pullman dislikes so much about the Church? What is your opinion of Pullman's portrayal of God, the "Authority"? Do you think there is any truth in some critics' comments that, due to Pullman's dislike of them, the clerics of the Magisterium are the only stereotyped characters in the trilogy?

18. William Blake wrote of John Milton, with specific regard to *Paradise Lost*, that he was "of the Devil's party without knowing it" (*The Marriage of Heaven and Hell*). Pullman has claimed in interview to be knowingly of the Devil's party. What does he mean by this? What has this to do with his rewriting of the myth of the Fall, with Lyra as the new Eve? Lyra pledges at the very end of the trilogy to build the republic of heaven. How will this

republic differ from the kingdom of heaven believed in by the Magisterium, or the republic of heaven Lord Asriel battles to create? What is the basis for Lyra's republic and, arguably, Pullman's morality?

19. *His Dark Materials* engages with very large questions about existence, evil, sin, love and morality. How does the trilogy make its readers engage with such metaphysical issues? Do you think this has anything to do with Pullman's assertion that "Thou shalt not is soon forgotten, but Once upon a time lasts forever"?

Realism and Fantasy

20. Pullman has been described as working in a tradition of epic fantasy written for, or appealing to, children. *His Dark Materials* has been favorably compared to J. R. R. Tolkein's *The Lord of the Rings*, C. S. Lewis's *Chronicles of Narnia* and J. K. Rowling's more recent *Harry Potter* novels. If you know these series, how do you think Pullman's trilogy compares? Is he engaged in the same sort of writing?

21. Define "fantasy" writing. Do you think this aptly describes *His Dark Materials*? What is the relation of "fantasy" writing to "truth"? Are the terms mutually exclusive? Bear in mind the epigraph that Pullman uses for "The Harpies" chapter in *The Amber Spyglass*: "I hate things all fiction . . . There should always be some foundation of fact" (AS, p. 291). How does this quotation from the poet Lord Byron relate to the "The Harpies" chapter, and to the trilogy in general? In interview, Pullman said that "*Northern Lights* is not a fantasy. It's a work of stark realism." What do you think he meant by that? Why might he resist the label of a "fantasy" writer?

22. Within the trilogy exist several alternate worlds, and many thousands more are mentioned. The first world encountered in

Northern Lights is similar to our world, but it is, as Pullman puts it, "different in many ways." What are the differences between Lyra's Oxford and Will's Oxford? How do these cities co-exist? Pullman discusses the scientific notion of "phase space." He describes it as "the notional space which contains not just the actual consequences of the present moment, but all the possible consequences." How does this idea work as a metaphor for Pullman's artistic and moral vision? What does it say about the importance of choice?

Intertextuality

23. In his Acknowledgements, Pullman writes that "I have stolen ideas from every book I have ever read." What "stolen" ideas, themes and storylines can you identify in the trilogy? To which literary traditions do these link Pullman's work? Do you think that Pullman is "stealing"? What other words might you use to define his use of earlier texts?

24. In the Acknowledgements, Pullman names three specific "debts" that he owes to earlier writers—to the essay "On the Marionette Theatre" by Heinrich von Kleist, to John Milton's *Paradise Lost*, and to the works of William Blake. If you have read any of these, think about the ways in which Pullman has adapted or interacted with these texts. In what ways do reading them alongside Pullman enrich your understanding and experience of the trilogy?

25. As a reader of the trilogy, does it matter if you haven't read these "intertexts"? Do the story and themes stand on their own? How might this question relate to the different audiences that the books have (children and adults), and the different ways in which the trilogy can be read (for its story and for its themes)?

Children's Literature

26. *The Amber Spyglass* was the first children's novel to win a major literary prize—the Whitbread Award—in competition with books for adults. Coupled with the phenomenal success of J. K. Rowling's *Harry Potter* novels, the 1990s and 2000s have been seen as a new golden age for children's literature. What conditions might have made this come about? Is it to do with a handful of gifted writers? Or are there other explanations?

27. Part of the phenomenon of both the *Harry Potter* books and *His Dark Materials* is that adults read and appreciate them as much as children. What do you think it is about *His Dark Materials* that makes it so appealing to adults as well as children? Is this a different appeal to the one exerted by *Harry Potter*, or the same?

28. In various lectures, Pullman has made provocative comments about the differences between literature written for children and for adults. In his Carnegie Medal Acceptance Speech, for example, he said that "There are some themes, some subjects, too large for adult fiction; they can only be dealt with adequately in a children's book." In "Let's Write It in Red," he said that "children's books, [. . .] at this time in our literary history, open out on a wideness and amplitude—a moral and mental spaciousness—that adult fiction seems to have turned its back on." Do you think this is a fair analysis of the current literary scene? What is it about children's literature that might make it more suited to "a moral and mental spaciousness," "a wideness and amplitude"? Do you agree that this is what Pullman does in *His Dark Materials*?

29. *His Dark Materials* has already been cited by some critics as a series that will endure well beyond all of our lifetimes, and Lyra has been applauded as a character as memorable as Lewis Carroll's Alice. Do you think this will be the case?

Bibliography

WORKS BY PHILIP PULLMAN

Novels

The Haunted Storm. London: NEL, 1972.

Galatea. London: Victor Gollancz, 1978.

Count Karlstein illustrated by Diana Bryan. London: Chatto & Windus, 1982, Doubleday, 2002. New York: Random House, 2000.

The Ruby in the Smoke. Oxford: Oxford University Press, 1985. Revised edition Puffin 1987; Scholastic 1999. New York: Random House, 1994.

The Shadow in the North. Oxford: Oxford University Press, 1986 (first published as *The Shadow in the Plate*). Revised edition Penguin 1988; Scholastic 1999. New York: Random House, 1989.

Spring-Heeled Jack: A Story of Bravery and Evil illustrated by David Mostyn. London: Doubleday, 1989. New York: Knopf, 2002.

The Broken Bridge. London: Macmillan, 1990. New York: Random House, 1994.

How To Be Cool. London: Macmillan, 1990.

Count Karlstein or The Ride of the Demon Huntsman illustrated by Patrice Aggs. London: Doubleday, 1991. New York: Random House, 1996.

The Tiger in the Well. London: Penguin, 1991. Scholastic, 1999. New York: Random House, 1992.

The Butterfly Tattoo. London: Pan Macmillan, 1992. (Originally published as *The White Mercedes*). New York: Random House, 1988 (as *The White Mercedes*).

The New Cut Gang: Thunderbolt's Waxwork illustrated by Mark Thomas. London: Viking, 1994.

The Tin Princess. London: Penguin, 1994. Scholastic, 2000. New York: Random House, 1996.

The Firework Maker's Daughter illustrated by Nick Harris. London: Doubleday, 1995. New York: Scholastic, 2001.

The New Cut Gang: The Gas-Fitter's Ball illustrated by Mark Thomas. London: Viking, 1995.

Northern Lights. London: Scholastic, 1995. Published in the US as *The Golden Compass*. New York: Knopf, 1996.

The Wonderful World of Aladdin and the Enchanted Lamp illustrated by David Wyatt. London: Scholastic, 1995.

Clockwork or All Wound Up illustrated by Peter Bailey. London: Doubleday, 1996; Corgi Yearling, 1997. New York: Scholastic, 1998.

The Subtle Knife. London: Scholastic, 1997. New York: Knopf, 1998.

Mossycoat illustrated by Peter Bailey. London: Scholastic, 1998.

I Was a Rat . . . or The Scarlet Slippers illustrated by Peter Bailey. London: Doubleday, 1999. New York: Yearling Books, 2002.

The Amber Spyglass. London: Scholastic, 2000. New York: Knopf, 2000.

Puss in Boots illustrated by Ian Beck. London: Doubleday, 2000. New York: Knopf, 2001.

Lyra's Oxford. Oxford: David Fickling Books, 2003. New York: Knopf, 2003.

Plays

Sherlock Holmes and the Limehouse Horror. Walton-on-Thames: Thomas Nelson, 1992.

Frankenstein. Adapted from the novel by Mary Shelley. Oxford: Oxford University Press, 1990.

Miscellaneous

Using the Oxford Junior Dictionary: A Book of Exercises and Games, illustrated by Ivan Ripley. Oxford: Oxford University Press, 1979.

Ancient Civilizations, illustrated by Gary Long. Exeter: Wheaton, 1981.

"Invisible Pictures." *Signal*. 60 September 1989, pp. 160–86.

"The Moral's in the Story, Not the Stern Lecture." *Independent*. July 18, 1996.

"Let's Write It in Red: The Patrick Hardy Lecture." *Signal 85*. January 1998, pp. 44–62.

"Picture Stories and Graphic Novels." In Kimberley Reynolds and Nicholas Tucker, eds. *Children's Book Publishing Since 1945*. Aldershot: Scholar Press, 1998, pp. 110–32.

"The Dark Side of Narnia." *The Guardian*. October 1, 1998.

"An Introduction to . . . Philip Pullman." In James Carter, ed. *Talking Books: Children's Authors Talk About the Craft, Creativity and Process of Writing*. London: Routledge, 1999, pp. 178–95.

"Dreaming of Spires." *The Guardian*. 27 July 2002.

"The Responsible Storyteller." *The Guardian*. December 28, 2002.

Ed., and Introduction to *Detective Stories* illustrated by Nick Hardcastle. London: Kingfisher, 1998.

SELECT SECONDARY MATERIAL

Criticism and Reviews

Alderson, Brian. "Compass, Knife and Spyglass." *New York Times*. November 19, 2000.

Berman, Matt. "Heaven Can't Wait." *Times-Picayune (New Orleans)*. November 5, 2000.

Bird, Anne-Marie. "Dust, Dæmons and Soul States: Reading Philip Pullman's *His Dark Materials*." *British Association of Lecturers in Children's Literature Bulletin*. 7 (June 2000), pp. 3–12.

Blacker, Terence. "At the Cutting Edge of Good and Evil." *Mail on Sunday*. December 7, 1997.

Chrisafis, Angelique. "Edinburgh 2002: Pullman Lays Down a Moral Challenge for Writers." *Guardian*. August 12, 2002.

———. "Fiction Becoming Worthless, Says Author." *Guardian*. August 12, 2002.

Dederer, Claire. "Fantasy with Polar Bears." *Newsday*. November 12, 2000.

Dirda, Michael. "A World Elsewhere." *Washington Post*. May 5, 1996.

———. "The Edge of the World." *Washington Post*. August 3, 1997.

———. "The Amber Spyglass." *Washington Post*. October 29, 2000.

Eccleshare, Julia. "Rational Magic." *Guardian*. October 28, 2000.

Fitzherbert, Claudia. "This Author is Original and Also Dangerous." *Daily Telegraph*. January 23, 2002.

Hardyment, Christina. "Children's Books: Hip History and Fierce Fables." *Independent*. December 1, 1997.

Hitchens, Peter. "The Most Dangerous Author in Britain." *Mail on Sunday*. January 27, 2002.

———. "Karl Marx Would be Proud of Blair Smear Merchants." *Mail on Sunday*. June 9, 2002.

Humphrys, John. "An Atheists' Creed Could be the Saving of the Church." *Sunday Times*. August 18, 2002.

Hunt, Peter. "Philip Pullman." In *Children's Literature*. Oxford: Blackwell, 2001, pp. 113–5.

Jefferson, Margo. "On Writers and Writing: Harry Potter for Grown-Ups." *New York Times*. January 20, 2002.

Johnson, Sarah. "Narnia for the Nineties." *The Times*. October 18, 1997.

———. "His Dark Materials: The Subtle Knife." *The Times*. December 1, 1997.

———. "On the Dark Edge of Imagination." *The Times*. October 18, 2000.

Jones, Dudley. "Only Make-Believe? Lies, Fictions, and Metafictions in Geraldine McCaughrean's *A Pack of Lies* and Philip Pullman's *Clockwork*." *The Lion and the Unicorn*. 23:1. January 1999, pp. 86–96.

Jones, Nicolette. "The Garden of Earthly Delights." *Sunday Times*. October 29, 2000.

Kemp, Peter. "Master of His Universe." *Sunday Times*. October 19, 1997.

Langton, Jane. "What is Dust?." *New York Times*. May 19, 1996.

Lenz, Millicent. "Philip Pullman." In Peter Hunt and Millicent Lenz, *Alternative Worlds in Fantasy Fiction*. London: Continuum, 2001, pp. 122–69.

Loer, Stephanie. "Author's Trilogy Inspired by Milton's 'Paradise Lost.'" *Boston Globe*. December 3, 2000.

Lyall, Sarah. "The Man Who Dared Make Religion the Villain." *New York Times*. November 7, 2000.

Maguire, Gregory. "Children's Books." *New York Times*. April 19, 1998.

Mann, Jessica. "A Paradise Without God." *Sunday Telegraph*. November 5, 2000.

Marr, Andrew. "Pullman Does for Atheism What C. S. Lewis Did for God." *Daily Telegraph*. January 24, 2002.

McCrum, Robert. "The World of Books: Pullman Gives his Readers Precisely the Satisfactions they Look for in a Novel." *Observer*. October 22, 2000.

———. "Dæmon Geezer." *Observer*. January 27, 2002.

McDonagh, Melanie. "Once Upon a Time, Children's Books were Looked Down On." *Daily Telegraph*. April 13, 2002.

Mckay, Carla. "Tempted by this Dark Spirited Fantasy." *Daily Mail*. December 1, 2000.

Nikolajeva, Maria. "Children's, Adult, Human . . . ?" In Sandra L Beckett, ed. *Transcending Boundaries: Writing for a Dual Audience of Children and Adults*. New York: Garland Publishing, 1999, pp. 63–80.

Rustin, Susanna. "Heaven is a Place on Earth." *Financial Times*. November 4, 2000.

Said, S. F. "Why Philip Pullman Should Win the Whitbread Tonight." *Daily Telegraph*. January 22, 2002.

Spencer, Charles. "The National's New Adventurer." *Daily Telegraph*. January 21, 2003.

Tonkin, Boyd. "An Inevitable Victory for a Dark and Complex Fable." *Independent*. January 23, 2002.

———. "Once Upon a Time in the Marketing Department . . ." *Independent*. November 6, 2002.

Thorpe, Nick. "The Anti-Christian Fundamentalist." *Sunday Times*. August 4, 2002.

Wagner, Erica. "Divinely Inspired." *The Times*. October 18, 2000.

———. "Courageous and Dangerous: A Writer for All Ages." *The Times*. January 23, 2002.

Walter, Natasha. "A Moral Vision for the Modern Age." *Independent*. January 24, 2002.

Warner, Marina. "Epilogue." *Fantastic Metamorphoses, Other Worlds: Ways of Telling the Self*. Oxford: Oxford University Press, 2002, pp. 207–12.

Wartofsky, Alona. "The Last Word." *Washington Post*. February 19, 2001.

Wood, N. "Paradise Lost and Found: Obedience, Disobedience, and Storytelling in C. S. Lewis and Philip Pullman." *Children's Literature in Education*. 32:4, pp. 237–59.

Interviews

Carey, Joanna. "The Pullman Engine." *Guardian*. April 23, 1996.

Costa, Maddy. "Kid's Stuff." *Guardian*. August 22, 2001.

de Bertodano, Helena. "I am of the Devil's Party." *Sunday Telegraph*. January 27, 2002.

Dickson, E Jane. "Telling Stories." *The Times*. June 2, 2001.

Feay, Suzi. "A Winner—If He Gets His Evil Way." *Independent on Sunday*. August 19, 2001.

Hardyment, Christina. "Grown-Up Talent in the Juvenile World." *Independent*. July 6, 1996.

Jones, Nicolette. "What Shall We Tell the Children?." *The Times*. July 18, 1996.

Kellaway, Kate. "A Wizard with Words." *Observer*. October 22, 2000.

Parsons, Wendy, and Nicholson, Catriona. "Talking to Philip Pullman: An Interview." *The Lion and the Unicorn*. 23:1 January 1999, pp. 116–34.

Potton, Ed. "Garden-Shed Visionary." *The Times*. January 24, 2002.

Robinson, Karen. "Dark Art of Writing Books That Win Minds." *Sunday Times*. January 27, 2002.

Ross, Deborah. "The Deborah Ross Interview: Philip Pullman: Soap and the Serious Writer." *Independent*. February 4, 2002.

Sharkey, Alix. "Heaven, Hell, and the Hut at the Bottom of the Garden." *Independent on Sunday*. December 6, 1998.

Stanistreet, Michelle. "Bestseller Philip Pullman Told Dark Tales Even as a Boy." *Sunday Express*. March 17, 2002.

Tucker, Nicholas. "Paradise Lost and Freedom Won." *Independent*. October 28, 2000.

Vincent, Sally. "Driven by Dæmons." *Guardian*. November 10, 2001.

Wavell, Stuart. "The Lost Children." *Sunday Times*. November 11, 2001.

Welch, Frances. "Jesus was like the Buddha and Galileo." *Sunday Telegraph*. November 19, 2000.

Websites

www.bbc.co.uk/arts/books/author/pullman

www.bbc.co.uk/radio4/arts/hisdarkmaterials

www.bookcollection.i8.com

www.bridgetothestars.net

www.darkmaterials.com

www.geocities.com/darkadamant

www.hisdarkmaterials.org

www.randomhouse.com/features/pullman (the US publisher's website)

www.robotwisdom.com/jorn/pullman.html

tts.inkypot.com (a His Dark Materials role-playing game)